SYNDROME S

SYNDROME **S**

HOW TO AVOID, MANAGE, AND REVERSE THE NEGATIVE HEALTH EFFECTS OF **STRESS**

Daniel Crisafi, ND, PhD

CHAT_{INC}

Published in the United States by CHAT Inc

Library of Congress Cataloging-in-Publication Data
Crisafi, Daniel
Syndrome S / Daniel Crisafi
Includes bibliographical references and index.
1. Health 2. Wellness 3. Stress 4. Nutrition 5. Crisafi, Daniel 6. Title

Trade Paperback ISSN: 978-0-9914620-0-1
e-Book ISSN: 978-0-9914620-1-8

Printed in Canada

Dedication

I'd like to dedicate this book to the one person who has had an important positive effect on every aspect of my life—professional, paternal, emotional, and, yes, sentimental.

To Suzie Rousseau, my wife.

Per sempre tuo.

Please Note

The information in this book is for educational purposes only. It should not be viewed as recommendations to diagnose or treat illness. All health matters should be supervised by a qualified healthcare professional. You should never attempt to decrease your use of prescription medication without first consulting with your physician. You should also inform your physician of any dietary supplements you are taking. The publisher and the author are not responsible for individuals who choose to self-diagnose, self-treat, or use the information in this book without consulting with their own healthcare practitioner.

Contents

Acknowledgements

THIS BOOK IS THE FRUIT of almost three decades of reflection on the impact stress has on human health. Those three decades have been influenced by a variety of people and experiences. And since I cannot name everyone who has played a meaningful role in helping to develop my professional, as well as personal, thoughts, I do want to acknowledge a few people who have been instrumental to the writing of this book. If you are one of those important people who are not mentioned, please accept my sincere apologies.

Knowledge, if it is to be of any use, must be practical and not just theoretical. Of course, the development of this book began nearly 30 years ago as I worked with patients on a daily basis. To each of my patients, I want to offer my sincere thanks. Indeed, I have learned more from you than I have from any of the courses I have taken, the seminars I have attended, or the books I have read.

My friends and peers in the natural health industry, in the Americas as well as in Europe, Asia, and Oceania, have always been a source of information, motivation, and intellectual growth. You certainly deserve to be acknowledged.

This book would not have been possible without the encouragement of several individuals, including Matthew James, president of Purity Life Health Products, and Albert Dahbour, vice-president of Wakunaga of America. Thank you Matthew for your 20-plus years of friendship and professional support. The conversation we had at dinner, with your lovely wife Julie and my beautiful blonde, Suzie, was instrumental in getting me to write this book. Albert, thanks for the wonderful products your company manufactures, especially Aged Garlic Extract. Thanks also for the generous amounts of time and money that Wakunaga has invested in solid scientific research. And, of course, thanks for your friendship and continued support.

Karolyn Gazella, a consummate writer and publisher, has been both supportive and patient through the writing of this book. Thank you. I also want to acknowledge the exceptional editorial support of Miriam Weidner and Deirdre Shevlin Bell.

I would be remiss if I didn't mention our pH Santé Beauté team: Nancy, Bessie, and Pauline. Bessie and Pauline, in particular, were instrumental in juggling my schedule so that I might finish this book (almost) within the established timeline.

Finally, to Suzie, my beloved, as well as to my four children, Genevieve, Jonathan, David, and Philippe: I offer my gratitude for your patience during those times when I needed to study and work—sometimes at the cost of spending time with you. Suzie, you have provided constant and unwavering support, both morally and intellectually. Thank you for being there.

Foreword

THE NEGATIVE IMPACTS OF STRESS are real, ubiquitous, and often devastating. Unfortunately and too often, however, biochemical and physiological effects of stress are overlooked. Although we can observe and feel personal stress effects day-to-day, we rarely examine the cumulative effects of stress. Stress can wreak havoc on many body systems: gastrointestinal, psychological, cardiovascular, hormonal, immunologic, behavioral, and energetic.

The basis of science is that every effect has a cause. If you experience a health problem today and did not have it last year, there is a reason. Changes in diet or in exercise levels can sometimes explain health symptoms, but those are not always an explanation for physiological changes. The same is true of aging.

This book will examine the major role of stress in a variety of disorders. However, we are not referring to the common and imprecise terminology of "feeling stressed." Nor are we talking about psychological stress, because much has been written about that—maybe too much. We are referring to how stressors affect the way the body works—the physiological impacts of stress.

I do not deny important psychological and spiritual aspects related to stress. This book, however, will focus on the biochemical and physiological aspects of stress. This emphasis has been significantly overlooked in stress-themed health content. I focus on these physical aspects because many of my patients, though balanced psychologically and spiritually, still suffer from the effects of stress. Stress is not only a matter of head or heart!

The term stress was coined by endocrinologist and Nobel Prize nominee Hans Selye, MD, in 1936. He defined stress as "the non-specific response of the body to any demand for change." Whenever the body is challenged by change, it experiences stress. Our reaction to this stress, known as the "fight or flight" response, is a built-in reaction designed to ensure our survival. When faced with danger, humans experience a complex chain of biological changes that instantly put us on alert. It begins in the hypothalamus, a tiny cluster of cells at the base of the brain that controls all automatic body functions. The hypothalamus triggers nerve cells to release norepinephrine, a hormone that tightens the muscles and sharpens the senses. At the same time, the adrenal glands release epinephrine, better known as adrenaline, which makes the heart pump faster and the lungs work harder to flood the body with oxygen. The adrenal glands also release the hormone cortisol, which helps the body convert sugar to energy. Once the threat has passed, the parasympathetic branch of the autonomic nervous system takes over, allowing the body to return to normal.

But, unlike our ancestors, who only had to deal with the occasional saber-toothed tiger or club-wielding enemy, we are often subjected to 50 or more stressors a day. Unfortunately, our bodies can't make the distinction between the life-threatening events like a fire and the frustration of being stuck in a traffic jam. Add in an undercurrent of worry from things that are beyond our control, and we rarely get a break from stress.

The problem is that stress impacts more than just our mental well-being. It can increase blood pressure, blood sugar, and sugar cravings. Over time, in can elevate unhealthy cholesterol and reduce your body's ability to detoxify itself, digest food, and sleep. Continually elevated stress hormones can also decrease bone formation, alter your pain threshold, and interfere with proper intestinal activity, reproduction, and wound repair.

Interestingly, Dr. Selye showed that the body responds to both good and bad stress in very similar ways. He also demonstrated that both physical and psychological stress cause very real physical symptoms by disrupting the way our nervous system and endocrine glands react. We cannot (and wouldn't want to) eliminate some stressors, and others can only be eliminated gradually. Still, we can engage in ways of helping the body deal with stress more effectively. These ways will minimize the damage stress causes to our bodies and our lives. With more knowledge and information, we can help minimize the price our bodies pay during times of stress.

It's not stress that kills us, it is our reaction to it.

— *Hans Selye*

FOR THE PHYSICIAN

This book is written for the consumer, not the healthcare professional. That said, the health professional can certainly benefit from information contained herein. I have intentionally used everyday language to make the information accessible to everyone. Though

I do not use scientific jargon, the book's content is based on solid scientific facts.

To the doctors reading this book: If what you read seems to counter what you were taught in medical school, I invite you consider the following quote by Nobel Prize laureate Max Planck. Think also of your patients suffering the physiological impacts of stress—some led to despair by impacts on quality of life. Remember that it's not "all in their heads!"

> *Scientific truth does not triumph by convincing its opponents and making them see the light, but rather because its opponents eventually die and a new generation grows up that is familiar with it.*
>
> — *Max Planck*

Introduction

THIS BOOK IS NOT ABOUT ME. It is about those individuals who are seeing their lives—or the lives of their loved ones, coworkers, and friends—negatively impacted by stress. As a certified naturopath (or as designated in my home province of Quebec, a *naturopathe agrée*), I have seen how stress can impact the health and well-being of the patients who come to see me.

This realization, however, took many years to come to fruition. I originally began my academic career studying philosophy and theology—two fields that still capture my interest. I also became a personal trainer and judo competitor at the national level. It seemed as though my life was on track and stress was the last thing I was concerned with. But then I experienced a serious health problem that challenged me to not only change my habits, but also my academic focus. I turned to natural approaches, a healthful diet, and supplements to manage my health. As I got better, I became interested in natural wellness as a career, obtaining a degree as a Master Herbalist and a PhD in nutrition with a specialty in nutritional biochemistry.

Along with establishing a vibrant private practice in Montreal, I have traveled extensively to lecture across the United States and Canada, as well as in the United Kingdom, Portugal, Spain, Malaysia, and New Zealand. I've also written books (*The Probiotic Approach*, *Candida Albicans*, *La Phytothérapie*,

Herbalism, and *Les Superaliments* with Sam Graci), contributed a chapter to Brad King and Dr. Michael Schmidt's book *Bio-Age*, and authored several condition-specific booklets for *Better Nutrition* magazine, including *Metabolic Syndrome* and *Blood Pressure*. Yet the importance of stress in overall health still eluded me.

It wasn't until my wife Suzie, an esthetician who believes that skin problems are more than skin deep, and I joined forces to establish an esthetic and naturopathic clinic that that I began to fully appreciate how stress can affect the body and the mind. Through the years, I began to see that a large percentage of patients who walked into the pH Santé Beauté clinic had symptoms that developed following periods of either acute intense stress or chronic stress. I also realized that nothing was being done to help them understand, and eliminate, the harmful effects of this stress.

In the chapter that follows, I'll share real stories of patients with a variety of health complaints. While their cases were all unique, they did have one thing in common: they were all suffering from negative physiological effects of stress. I call this collection of impacts "Syndrome S." As you'll read, Syndrome S symptoms vary depending on the patient and his or her particular situation. All of the patients, however, present symptoms that any of us can experience given the "right" circumstances and lifestyles.

CHAPTER ONE

Sneaky Stress and Syndrome S

FOR MOST OF HER ADULT LIFE, Cathy was a fairly typical middle-aged professional. She enjoyed a rewarding career and, most important to her, a happy family life. Cathy seemed to be the perfect wife, mother, and professional. She was also in great physical shape and a pretty good weekend athlete to boot. Cathy's friends called her "Superwoman" because of the way she excelled without even seeming to try.

When I first met Cathy at my clinic, however, the person I examined was far from the superwoman of a few years before. Cathy shared a bit about her declining health in the past few years, but mainly focused on what was bothering her most: insomnia and an irritable bowel diagnosis.

Her sleep problems started gradually and insidiously. When we met, Cathy complained that she would generally fall asleep well unless she was experiencing stress. When stressed, however, it might take her an hour or more to fall asleep. And even when she didn't "feel" stressed her sleep was gradually worsening.

Cathy would wake a few times each night, her brain reeling with real or perceived problems and solutions. Sleep was a big issue because she realized her energy during the day declined along with her ability to sleep soundly. Her focus and memory were also negatively affected. Cathy was tiring both physically and mentally due to lack of quality sleep.

Her irritable bowel issue had also developed gradually. At first she had gas and bloating, more than previously and without necessarily having eaten those foods we associate with gastro-intestinal symptoms. Over time Cathy started feeling bloated no matter what she ate. In fact, she often complained of feeling three months pregnant by the end of the day. Stress levels also affected her bowel activity; she experienced occasional constipation and frequent loose stools or diarrhea.

Cathy's consulting physician referred her to a gastroenter-ologist. The standard medical tests, including a colonoscopy, gave no indication of anything abnormal. Eventually, Cathy was given a diagnosis of irritable bowel. Now bear in mind that irritable bowel is a diagnosis of exclusion. This means that when a patient has certain symptoms, such as gas, bloat-ing, diarrhea, and/or constipation, and a physician can't find anything abnormal, he or she usually gives a diagnosis of "irritable bowel."

While quizzing Cathy on the initial triggers preceding her symptoms, I discovered that the most were related to stress. Within a period of a few years, she had to deal with the prover-bial "drops that make the bucket overflow." She had become caregiver to her dying mother, learned of her husband's affair with a coworker, and managed the emotional difficulties of her teenage son. Superwoman had finally met her match.

Since Cathy's symptoms seem to have been triggered by a series of stressors, she was told that her symptoms were stress-related. They certainly were, but the prescription was no more helpful than the suggestion she "get a life" and deal with these normal life events. If she couldn't pull it together herself, her doctor recommended sleeping pills or antidepressants.

Unfortunately, Cathy's situation (and her treatment) is quite common. I've seen hundreds of patients with similar issues, and I can tell you that antidepressants are not the answer. Cathy was living the physiological effects of Syndrome S.

STEALTH STRESS SYMPTOMS

Jerry was a mid-40s lawyer who seemed healthy enough when he came to my clinic. He told me, "I don't have any health problems; I just want to lose weight." His weight, which had averaged 170 pounds for at least two decades, had increased to 220 in three years. Jerry didn't understand. He hadn't really changed his diet or level of activity within that period. He couldn't understand the extra pounds that had increased so gradually.

I saw that Jerry's weight increase had largely been around his belly—what we call abdominal fat. Both of us knew he had to do something about his weight or live with an increase in the risk of heart disease.

When I reviewed Jerry's blood tests, I noticed that though his cholesterol and blood sugar were normal, the numbers had been gradually and consistently increasing. Indeed, if the trend continued, Jerry would soon have diagnosable cholesterol and blood sugar issues.

As we continued to talk, several other symptoms came to light. Jerry said that his libido had recently decreased. Though he still found his wife very attractive, his sex drive was much lower than what it had been before he started noticing the weight increase. Jerry also used the term "plagued" to describe his salt cravings. He shared that few things brought him as much comfort as snacking on pretzels or chips, especially at the end of the workday.

When I asked about his stress levels, Jerry admitted that he was more "trigger happy." "It takes less and less to blow my lid," he confessed. "My kids are really getting blasted, sometimes for nothing." Additionally, although he said the other attorneys hadn't yet noticed, Jerry was having more difficulty dealing with the normal law firm operations.

Jerry noticed these behavioral symptoms seemed to have developed following a series of stressors: increased professional responsibility after his promotion to full partner, a divorce and relatively quick remarriage, and the financial stress related to both.

Though his primary physician had not given a specific diagnosis, he had warned Jerry about the weight gain and its potential long-term side effects, and rightfully so. Jerry's collection of symptoms also indicated a case of Syndrome S.

STRESS AND HORMONE HAVOC

Pat was an auto dealership clerk in her mid-30s. A good-humored, well-balanced person, she could take what the automobile sales staff and mechanics could dish out, which was not an easy task. Pat came to me for a problem very different from Cathy's or Jerry's. Pat had significant premenstrual problems, including migraines, water retention, breast pain, and significant mood changes. Pat also developed hypothyroidism, a condition marked by an ineffective thyroid gland.

Pat also was trying to get pregnant and could not. Though hypothyroidism can lead to problems with fertility, the fertility problems first began while Pat's hormone levels seemed to be normal. As a general rule Pat didn't have emotional challenges except during PMS or when she skipped a meal. Indeed, some of Pat's symptoms seemed to be triggered by or worsened by the need to eat. If Pat was hungry, but unable to eat, her symptoms often got worse, especially her "hyper-reactivity."

Pat's physician believed some of her symptoms were a result of her inability to get pregnant. To be sure, though Pat and her partner Michael had a wonderful relationship, their inability to have children seemed to be a major hurdle in the couple's well-being. But this was not the real reason behind Pat's issues. Her physiological and emotional issues were connected and a result of the effects of Syndrome S.

PSYCHOLOGICAL STRESS IMPACTS PHYSIOLOGY

Luke was a very successful actor with a witty sense of humor and a sharp intelligence that masked the significant amount of stress he struggled with all his life. This young man, for whom family was everything, was raised in a loving, tight-knit, conservative family. In the mid-1990s Luke realized his homosexuality. He initially decided to hide this from both his parents and childhood friends. The stress of being in the closet with those he loved had tremendous negative effects.

The drop that made the (stress) bucket overflow happened when Luke's mother, the person he cherished most, died in a car accident. This wonderfully gifted actor, recognized by both the public and peers, started suffering from anxiety and full-blown panic attacks. These attacks tended to occur when stress was especially high.

Once, before a major award ceremony, his stress level increased to the point where he was unable to attend and accept the award. As the symptoms worsened, Luke had to actively manage his stress before filming episodes of his TV show. Unfortunately, this preparation involved combining an antianxiety drug with one or two glasses of wine. The combination calmed Luke's anxiety because, along with being a psychological response, Luke's stress was also a biochemical reaction triggered by continually high cortisol levels. But, while this sedating ritual allowed Luke to avoid panic attacks, the drug and alcohol fog caused him to forget his lines. Ultimately, Luke was fired from the show—another victim of Syndrome S.

IT'S NOT JUST "IN YOUR HEAD"

In more than two decades I have seen thousands of patients with a wide variety of symptoms developed during or after periods of stress. In many cases these symptoms drove a significant reduction in quality of life. In a few cases the symptoms led to deep despair. In every case, the prior diagnosis had been nervous tension, burnout, anxiety, or depression. These diagnoses result in missed opportunities to deal positively with physiological issues and improve overall health.

If these stories sound familiar, and if the effects of stress have impacted you or a loved one, please read on. I'll show you that stress has real physiological effects. I'll also share the good news that most, if not all, of these effects can be reversed with nutritional and lifestyle shifts. Most importantly, I'll give you the information you need to make these positive shifts for your own life.

CHAPTER TWO

The Causes and Meaning of Stress

WHEN I TALK TO PATIENTS ABOUT STRESS, I start by sharing a clear definition. A patient of mine once claimed her symptoms couldn't be due to stress. She said her life was well balanced, she had a wonderful husband, and her children were "good kids." She couldn't identify any major trauma or stressor in her life, but she was nonetheless experiencing Syndrome S–type symptoms. When we start to look at all the types of potential stress, we usually identify aspects of life the patient had not recognized as "stress."

The concept of stress, a result of the adaptive efforts of the body, has been popularized in large part through the work of Nobel Prize laureate Hans Selye. His seminal book *The Stress of Life* highlighted the fact that stress is normal, even beneficial. The body, according to Selye, can adapt to stress as long as the stress is not too great and adaptive body mechanisms have not been reduced in any way.

In his book, *Treat the Cause*, Peter Papadogianis highlights the fact that a variety of types of stressors exist, such as physical, emotional, professional, social, and chemical. As a matter of fact, anything that elicits a response from the body—that forces your body to react—can be considered a stressor. As Selye wrote, a stressor therefore is demand that elicits a nonspecific response in the body. Others have defined a stressor as any condition or stimulus that disrupts the homeostatic balance in the body.

For my patients and in my work, I define stress in the following ways:

- Physical, chemical, or emotional factors that causes bodily or mental tension.
- Any change that requires mental, physiological, or biochemical adaptation.

These stressors can be catalogued into two general categories: eustress and distress. We often forget or discount eustress for reasons you'll see below.

Eustress is "good stress," without which an individual cannot improve or grow. One good example of eustress is exercise. After exercise, the body responds to stress by adapting. Muscle and bone tissue are increased to meet the accrued demand (stress) made upon them. The exercise leads to changes, such as muscle growth, that help the body. Eustress can also be the kind of rush we get during a deadline. The body helps manage the situation by becoming more alert and focused. In many cases, we become more challenged and motivated. In general, eustress is not typically what we mean when we say, "I'm so stressed!"

Distress is the kind of stress that we would generally consider "bad stress" from a physiological point of view. Distress is stress that is too much to bear or cope with. Examples include the death of a loved one, the loss of a job, absorption of toxic chemicals, or sensory overload. These are types of stress we typically want to avoid. Physiologically, we feel an increase in blood pressure, breath rate, and generalized tension. We may turn to negative behavioral coping mechanisms, such as over-eating, smoking, or drinking too much.

I maintain that from a psychological and spiritual perspective, we should avoid labeling any stressor as "bad stress." As human beings we may become better because of both eustress and distress. We can grow and build character through the process. From a physiological perspective, however, distresses are always bad. These stressors elicit response without leading to any positive physiological or biochemical change. We do not better ourselves because of distress; we must better ourselves in spite of it.

The key to this positive result is stress tolerance, or the power to endure stress and manage the symptoms of stress. Because the body and mind are connected, any work toward managing the psychological symptoms of stress will improve any physiological symptoms.

Of course, the first step in managing stress is to identify its origins.

SOCIAL READJUSTMENT RATING SCALE

One way I help patients put stress into perspective is to use a scale called the Social Readjustment Rating Scale. This scale was developed in the late 1960s at the University of Washington School of Medicine by researchers Thomas Holmes and Richard Rahe. Their key objective in developing the scale was to provide a way to measure the impact of common life stressors. Many decades later, this scale is still recognized as a bona fide tool in assessing stressors.

Take a few moments to sum the values for recent stressors in your own life. How far back in time you go depends on your personal reaction to stressors. It's wise to take the following factors into consideration when reviewing the following chart: how reactive you are to stress from a genetic point of view (do you come from a long line of "worriers?"), whether or not you experienced past physical or emotional trauma, and the state of your hormonal balance. Other factors, including the quality of your diet, whether or not you exercise or practice relaxation therapy, and your spiritual beliefs can also play a role in how you react to stress, physically, mentally, and emotionally.

LIFE EVENT	VALUE
Death of spouse	100
Divorce	73
Marital separation	65
Jail term	63
Death of close family member	63
Personal injury or illness	53
Marriage	50
Fired at work	47
Marital reconciliation	45
Retirement	45
Change in health of family member	44
Pregnancy	40
Sex difficulties	39
Gain of new family member	39
Business readjustment	39
Change in financial state	38
Death of close friend	37
Change to a different line of work	36
Change in number of arguments with spouse	35
Home Mortgage over $100,000*	31
Foreclosure on mortgage or loan	30

Change in responsibilities at work	29
Son or daughter leaving home	29
Trouble with in-laws	29
Outstanding personal achievement	28
Spouse begins or stops work	26
Begin or end school	26
Change in living conditions	25
Revision of personal habits	24
Trouble with boss	23
Change in work hours or conditions	20
Change in residence	20
Change in schools	20
Change in recreation	19
Change in church activities	19
Change in social activities	18
Mortgage or loan of less than $100,000*	17
Change in sleeping habits	16
Change in number of family get-togethers	15
Change in eating habits	15
TOTAL	

* Mortgage figure was updated from the original figure of $10,000 to reflect inflation.

INTERPRETING YOUR RESULTS

Though no test of this kind is flawless, it is still a useful tool to assess the cumulative impacts of stress over time. A total of 150 or less is an indicator that your stress level is not high. If your score is 150 to 299, the chances are about 50 percent that you will develop stress-related symptoms. If your score is 300 or higher, you stand an almost 80 percent chance of developing stress-related symptoms.

Beyond using this scale as a tool, I want to highlight two concepts: First, the impact of stress is cumulative. What Holmes and Rahe discovered is how stressors from the past can contribute to how effectively we deal with current stresses. Within earlier case studies, I mentioned the drop that makes the bucket overflow. The final breakdown is a result of cumulative and progressive stress. This is also why many of my patients are surprised by how a seemingly minor stress can sometimes trigger important symptoms. Our bucket, so to speak, has gradually filled up. It therefore takes only a drop or two to cause an overflow.

The second concept I want to highlight is that positive life events can affect the body negatively and with a similar score to so called "bad stressors." Marriage, for example, has a similar score to personal injury or illness and being fired from work. Although marriage should be a wondrously happy event, it rates quite high as a stressor. Recall Luke who had a panic attack the evening of his award ceremony. The Homes and Rahe scale scores "Outstanding personal achievement" as 28. That's almost as stressful as "Foreclosure on mortgage or loan" or "Trouble with in-laws."

The following story provides a good example of both concepts. Dorothy developed a variety of symptoms after a move from Atlanta to New Haven. She had wanted to move to New Haven for years to be closer to her son, Tom, who was teaching at Yale. She and her husband also saw New Haven as a more comfortable retirement choice, especially with a grandchild on the way.

Dorothy, however, started developing certain symptoms as the date of the move grew close. Her sleep was not sound and she increasingly complained of intermittent headaches and abdominal pain. Finally, Dorothy began to have heart palpitations, especially at night, and her sleep worsened all the more. Why would such positive changes bring on these symptoms? This is where the cumulative effect of stress as indicated by Social Readjustment Scores can come in handy. Let's calculate the past stressors that Dorothy had experienced, taking into account the factors of genetics, hormones, and lifestyle discussed above. Because of Dorothy's reaction to stressors and the fact that stress can have a cumulative effect, we looked at all the events that occurred during her adult life.

YEAR	DOROTHY'S LIFE EVENT	CUMULATIVE SCORE
1974	Dorothy is accepted at university, she has to move to another state. Begin or end school = 26 points. Change of residence = 20 points.	46
1977	Dorothy gets her degree, moves back home, and begins a new job. She ends school = 26 points; changes her social activities (leaves her college friends) = 18 points.	44
1980	Dorothy marries Peter. They move into a small apartment. Marriage = 50 points. Change in residence = 20 points.	70

1983	Dorothy becomes pregnant. Pregnancy = 40 points.	40
1984	Dorothy and her husband gain a new family member, Tom. Gain of a new family member = 39 points.	39
2004	Tom leaves for college on a scholarship. Son or daughter leaving home = 29 points.	29
2009	Amidst the banking and mortgage crisis Peter loses his job, causing a significant change in their financial state. Spouse begins or stops work = 26. Change in financial state = 38 points.	64
2012	Dorothy's mother is diagnosed with breast cancer. Change in health of family member = 44.	44
2013	Dorothy and Peter move to New Haven. Change in residence = 20.	20
TOTAL		**396**

Of course, there's nothing excessive about any of these stressors, and they are very common in life. Still, with a score of almost 400, Dorothy stands an almost 80 percent chance of developing stress-related symptoms. Simple stressors that most of us go through can build up, gradually and insidiously. At some point, our bodies just can't take any more. That's when we develop Syndrome S.

The Social Readjustment Rating Scale is a helpful tool to understand what stress is and how it can gradually cause troubling symptoms. The scale does not, however, address two extremely important concepts for discussion. The scale does not include hormonal or environmental stressors in the list. Furthermore, the scale provides absolute scores and cannot adjust for individual capacity to deal with stress. Every individual has unique capacities for stress tolerance. And even beyond these innate characteristics, we can each make choices to increase or decrease management of stress symptoms.

CHAPTER THREE

The Physiology of Stress

THE NOTION OF STRESS AND PHYSIOLOGICAL EFFECTS IS NOT NEW. Indeed, many studies have reported the insidious effects of stress on the body as well as the mind. A quick look at the American Psychological Association (APA) 2010 report, Stress in America Findings, provides a list of physical symptoms generally attributed to stress. The chart below lists these symptoms.

SYMPTOMS OF STRESS

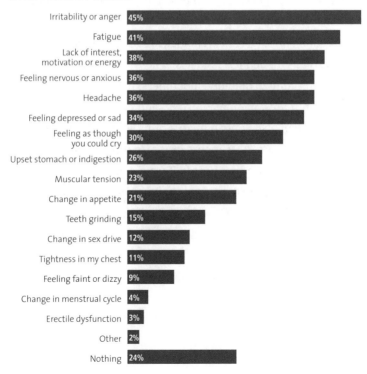

Symptom	Percentage
Irritability or anger	45%
Fatigue	41%
Lack of interest, motivation or energy	38%
Feeling nervous or anxious	36%
Headache	36%
Feeling depressed or sad	34%
Feeling as though you could cry	30%
Upset stomach or indigestion	26%
Muscular tension	23%
Change in appetite	21%
Teeth grinding	15%
Change in sex drive	12%
Tightness in my chest	11%
Feeling faint or dizzy	9%
Change in menstrual cycle	4%
Erectile dysfunction	3%
Other	2%
Nothing	24%

As might be expected from an APA report, this chart emphasizes the psychological dimensions of stress. It also includes a number of physical symptoms. Some authors have focused their examination of stress on its effects on the body in general, as well as specific impacts on blood sugar regulation. Psychiatrist Carl C. Pfeiffer describes stress-related symptoms (including those related to blood sugar) in his groundbreaking book, *Mental and Elemental Nutrients*.

"Later the symptoms may be many, but some of the most common somatic complaints are fatigue or exhaustion, headaches, heart palpitations, muscular aching or twitching, prickling or tingling of the skin, excessive sweating, gasping for breath, trembling, dizziness, weak spells, fainting, double or blurred vision, cold hands or feet, craving for sugar, hunger, chronic indigestion and nausea. Psychological symptoms include confusion, absent-mindedness, indecisiveness, loss of memory and/or concentration, irritability, moodiness, restlessness, insomnia, fears, nightmares, paranoia, anxiety and depression."

Stress can also contribute to a number of chronic diseases, as evidenced by a 2007 report in the *Journal of the American Medical Association* that noted, "Stress is involved as a causal factor in more than 80 percent of all non-infectious diseases." Following is another list, categorized by body system, that was developed by K.L. McCance and J. Shelby and featured in their book *Pathophysiology: The Biological Basis for Disease in Adults*. As you will see, it clearly underlines these findings.

CARDIOVASCULAR SYSTEM
Coronary artery disease
High blood pressure
Stroke

MUSCULOSKELETAL SYSTEM
Tension headaches
Muscle contraction
Backache

CONNECTIVE TISSUES
Rheumatoid arthritis and
related connective tissue
disorders

PULMONARY SYSTEM
Asthma
Hay fever

IMMUNE SYSTEM
Immunodepression
Autoimmune disease

GASTROINTESTINAL SYSTEM
Ulcer
Irritable bowel syndrome
Diarrhea
Nausea and vomiting
Ulcerative colitis

GENITOURINARY SYSTEM
Diuresis
Impotence
Frigidity

SKIN
Eczema
Acne

ENDOCRINE SYSTEM
Diabetes mellitus
Amenorrhea

CENTRAL NERVOUS SYSTEM
Fatigue and lethargy
Overeating
Depression
Insomnia

All lists aside, I want to emphasize an important point. If you suffer from one or any number of these symptoms, cannot identify a precipitating physical cause, and rate high in the stress scale, it's probable that stress has caused or exacerbated the problem. In Chapter 4, I provide a checklist to help you assess the role stress may play in your health problems.

CHAPTER FOUR

Stress Symptom Assessment

THIS CHAPTER IS INTENDED to help you assess whether stress plays a role in your health problems. I want you to see to what extent stress might be a factor, and I hope it will reassure you that it's not all in your head. In order to do this, you should revisit your social readjustment rating score in tandem with the System/ Symptom Questionnaire on the next page.

As you check off stress events on the scale, do not take into consideration whether you believe the stress affected you tangibly or not. In other words, it doesn't matter if you "felt" the stress. We are all affected differently and in many cases stress may affect us only biochemically and physiologically, in which case we often wouldn't be able to judge from our emotions.

Also, as I mentioned earlier, each individual stress may not have elicited reactions. Remember, the first 10,000 straws may not break the camel's back, but those pounds made the 10,001st one too many.

After you tally your score, move to the following questionnaire. Just check the symptoms for which you actually have symptoms. Of course, these symptoms may be due to a variety of other causes, not just stress. However, when standard medical exams can't find the cause of the problem, or when many of them seem to develop almost simultaneously, stress may be the cause.

The symptoms are listed by category. At the end of each category you can note the total yeses per category group, which will give you an indication that stress may affect certain body systems. This questionnaire is not cumulative the way the Social Readjustment Scale is. However, it does give a bird's eye view of symptoms that may be caused by stress and the group or groups that are most affected in your case. In later chapters, I'll share nutrition and lifestyle suggestions so you can work on those areas most affected both quickly and effectively.

STRESS SYSTEM/SYMPTOM QUESTIONNAIRE

BODY SYSTEM	SYMPTOM	YES
NEURO-MUSCULAR	Back pain	
	Carpal tunnel syndrome	
	Cervical (neck) pain	
	Cramps	
	Fibromyalgia	
	Grinding of teeth	
	Headaches	
	Lumbar pain	
	Muscle pain	
	Numbness or tingling (especially in the extremities)	
	Tiredness	
	Torticollis	
TOTAL		
RESPIRA-TORY	Asthma	
	Bronchial constriction	
	Difficulty breathing	
	Rhinitis	
TOTAL		
CARDIO-VASCULAR	Arrhythmia	
	Heart palpitations	
	High blood pressure	
	Migraines	
	Raynaud's syndrome	
	Tachycardia	
	Tinnitus	
TOTAL		

NEURO-PSYCHO-LOGICAL	Anxiety	
	Difficulty focusing (mentally)	
	Nervousness	
	Overreacting to stress	
	Panic attacks	
	Problems with concentration	
	Problems with memory	
	Vertigo	
	Waking up at night	
TOTAL		
GASTRO-INTESTINAL	Bloating	
	Burping	
	Constipation	
	Diarrhea	
	Duodenal ulcer	
	Gastritis	
	Indigestion	
	Reflux (heartburn)	
	Stomach ulcer	
	Ulcerative colitis	
TOTAL		
HAIR, NAILS, AND SKIN	Brittle hair	
	Brittle nails	
	Excessive sweating	
	Hair loss	
	Ridged nails	
	Vitiligo	
TOTAL		
HORMONAL	Decreased libido	
	Endometriosis	
	Infertility	
	Osteopenia or osteoporosis	
	Ovarian cysts	
	PMS	
	Premenstrual migraines	
TOTAL		
ADDICTIVE	Craving for sugar	
	Craving for salt	
	Craving for fat	
	Craving for alcohol	
TOTAL		
TOTAL ALL CATEGORIES		

FEAR AND LOVE

As we've established, the body reacts the same way to both "bad" and "good" stress. Without beleaguering the point, let's use the example of fear and love. Imagine someone very fearful; maybe they've been told that a certain individual is out to kill them and will be in town the next day. They'll probably lose their appetite. Who wouldn't? Sleep, of course, will be very difficult as they anxiously imagine a variety of scenarios for the upcoming day. And when they are finally confronted by the individual, they will probably get red and flushed in the face with sweaty palms.

Now imagine another scenario. It has probably happened to you. You meet someone you are very interested in. He or she returns your smile and may even hold your hand or embrace you. Your body, surprisingly, reacts the same as it would in a state of fear. You lose your appetite. Sleep is most difficult; you think about that person anxiously and expectantly. Finally, if he or she kissed you, you might get red and flushed in face and have very sweaty palms.

Fear or love, bad or good, the body reacts to stress in the same way. That is why both stressors can have the same impact on the body. Though psychologically there is no degree of commonality between falling in love and the fear of getting killed, the body nevertheless reacts in a similar manner.

CAVEMAN FIGHT OR FLIGHT

In Chapter 1, we examined stress reactions of five very different individuals. In all cases certain symptoms could be categorized as "nervous" or psychological. In many cases there were also very physical symptoms. We've also seen that the triggers can be very different.

Cathy was expected to burn the candle by both ends, being supermom, superwife, and superemployee. For Jerry, overwork was a factor, though his divorce also heavily influenced his stress level. Pat's stress symptoms seemed to come from the fact that she was unable to fulfill one of her life's ambitions—to have a baby. Finally, Luke even had a "stress reaction" to an overwhelmingly positive event, receiving an award. Why is this? What characteristic of the stress response can we target for such a wide variety of symptoms? Why does our body react to stress in such an excessive way?

When discussing stress, it helps to put a few things into perspective. When there is stress, whatever the stress, the body mobilizes itself to respond in an appropriate manner. It prepares itself physiologically to fight or to flee. It will reduce any function detrimental to fight or flight activities. The body also increases any reaction or function conducive to fight or flight. In other words, the body is wired or programmed to protect itself—to ensure survival, at almost any cost.

The problem, however, is that with most stressors today we just can't fight or flee. Imagine waking up in the morning and realizing there is no food in your cupboard and no money in your cookie jar. Your stress hormones increase as your body prepares itself for fight or flight. A hundred years ago you would respond to that stress by hunting, fishing, gathering, or stealing. In any case, you would use your body's stress mechanisms in your response. Unfortunately, most of us can't respond physically to that sort of situation anymore. Let's say you hate your job and hate a coworker. They continually harass you, and though you've complained to the competent authorities, nothing is being done for now. You can't leave your job, because that would be another important stress—no pay. A hundred years ago you might have solved the problem by using a baseball bat on your coworker. Unfortunately (or fortunately depending on where you stand), we can't to do that anymore. It's a good thing for social peace, but not a good thing for your body.

So, though we humans have not changed biochemically or physiologically, we have significantly changed socially. The body is still hardwired to fight or flee, but we can't give in to this physiological demand. That is part of the problem and what perpetuates stress effects.

Also, though we generally don't fight or flee anymore, we still eat as though we could and should. We have not adjusted our diets appropriately, and that also affects how stress impacts us. I discuss nutritional aspects of stress in later chapters.

WATER TORTURE

Especially in recent decades, we also have experienced significant changes in the intensity and frequency of stressors. In the past, we might have experienced intense stress, but for most people these stresses were not constant or prolonged. Today, stressors tend to be less intense, but they are far more frequent and some are constant. Our ancestors didn't have to deal with stress on a daily basis. The occasional stresses were intense indeed, but they were not everyday occurrences.

If there was no food, the body would mobilize for flight or fight, ready to do something physically. In response to this stress, individuals would go out and hunt. Once they killed the prey they would have food for some time (and no other immediate stress). In farming, the intense agricultural cycle led to stress for weeks, tilling the soil, sowing the seeds and waiting for the first hints of plant growth. However, once the crop began to grow, stress levels dropped. Once the crop was harvested, stress almost disappeared. Of course, I am oversimplifying the concept of stress intensity, but the point is that stressors were very intense, but not as sustained in the past as they are today.

In our day, physical, socioeconomic, and environmental stressors are very different. Most stresses are nowhere near as intense as those of our ancestors. While our stresses are relatively minimal, however, they are constant and debilitating. For most of us there's the stress of commuting to work, day in and day out. The stress of performance at work is in many ways different than it was in the past. Because most of life in the past had a physical component, the body was able to "use" fight or flight reactions. In most work environments today we can't fight or flee. You may not be frightened for your life, but there are continuous performance stressors that were only minimally present 200 years ago.

Furthermore, the addition of the most useful of tools—fax, e-mail, and smart phones—have led to response expectancies, which lead to greater stress. Today, someone may send you an e-mail telling you he needs certain non-urgent information. After a day or so he leaves a message on your smart phone and possibly sends another e-mail. Everything seems to be in emergency mode. What would he have done in the days before these useful tools were invented?

Today our life is fast-paced and buzzing with unending activity. Some believe we are being tortured slowly and continuously, just like the infamous water torture. One drop, two drops, three drops … finally after a few thousand drops, the insistent impact of each drop of water achieves its intended purpose, and we give in.

For us and with stress, "giving in" means a gradual break-down of the adrenal glands, digestive tract, thyroid, pancreas, and liver. As our body reacts to stress by mobilizing to fight or flee, our stress glands overreact too often and tire out. Many or all of Syndrome S symptoms begin with stress's impact on our adrenal glands.

CHAPTER FIVE

The Cortisol Connection

STRESS CAN NEGATIVELY AFFECT several glands and body systems. Earlier, I mentioned the adrenal glands, important glands that react physiologically to stress. Below, I'll explore adrenal function and how stress impacts function. I'll give a few practical examples of biochemical stress effects and cascading symptoms.

Bear with me now to review adrenal gland function with slightly more technical language. This table provides a bird's eye view of the complex biochemical adaptive mechanisms involved in the body's response to stress.

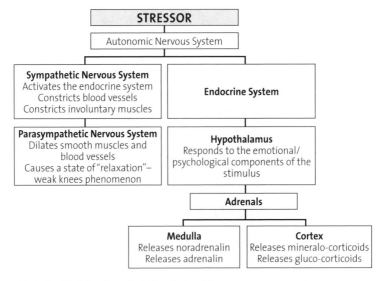

Adapted from The Kellogg Report (Bard College Center, 1989)

As we can see, the adrenal glands have a major role to play in the final phase of the stress response. The adrenal glands are two small glands that sit on top of the kidneys. They are also referred as suprarenal, literally translating to "above the kidneys."

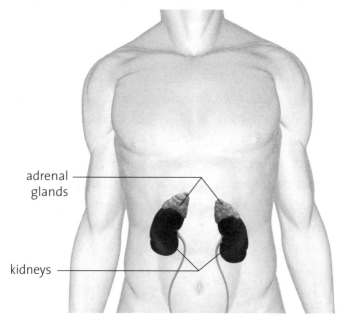

Adrenals consist of two parts, the medulla and the cortex. The adrenal medulla, the inner part of the gland, secretes epinephrine (a.k.a. adrenaline) and norepinephrine. The adrenal cortex, situated around the perimeter of the gland, secretes mineralocorticoids, glucocorticoids, and gonadocorticoids. Let's look at each part of the adrenal gland in more detail.

ADRENAL MEDULLA OVERVIEW

During stress and after stimulation by the sympathetic nervous system and the hypothalamus, the adrenal medulla secretes epinephrine (adrenaline) and norepinephrine (noradrenaline).

These help us cope with stress by increasing heart rate, blood pressure, oxygen consumption, and blood sugar levels. They also increase blood flow to the skeletal muscles. All these responses are in service of the fight or flight response. Epinephrine also prompts the release of pituitary hormones. The pituitary gland releases endorphins, natural narcotics that suppress immunity and reduce the perception of pain.

When your heart rate goes up and your blood pressure increases, blood is pumped more quickly to parts of the body required to fight or run. The increase in oxygen consumption and blood sugar gives us the extra energy required to deal with physical stress. The increase in endorphin release ensures that pain will not reduce our aggression or speed capabilities.

Runners go through this process every time they reach a certain level of intensity. The heart rate increases, skeletal muscles get more blood in order to respond more effectively to demand, and the natural narcotics, endorphins, reduce pain. You now know why many runners get what is termed "runner's high." The body doesn't know they are running for the health of it. In fact, some runners will say they are "addicted" to running. In a way, they are!

Now imagine someone under stress. His or her blood pressure and heart rate might increase. Under ongoing and continuous stress, with the adrenal medulla working overtime, blood pressure, heart rate, and blood sugar may remain elevated. This person may also experience muscle pain due to the increased and accrued blood sent to skeletal muscles. Ultimately, he or she may have more frequent infections or take more time to recover from infectious disease because of immunosuppressant endorphin effects. Are you starting to see a picture develop?

ADRENAL CORTEX OVERVIEW

During stress, and in response to the sympathetic nervous system via the hypothalamus, the adrenal cortex secretes mineralocorticoid and glucocorticoid hormones. Mineralocorticoids increase sodium reabsorption and elimination of potassium through the kidneys, thereby increasing water retention. The glucocorticoids increase blood sugar levels and inhibit inflammation and immune response. All of these physiological actions ensure that the body has an adequate supply of blood and glucose to provide the energy needed to either flee a dangerous situation or turn and fight.

The adrenal cortex also secretes gonadocorticoids (i.e., sex hormones). These are androgens (male hormones) and estrogens (female hormones). Current research is highlighting the fact that stress can have an impact on hormone production, affecting libido, PMS, and menopausal symptoms, as well as fertility. This impact is more evident when testosterone or estrogen production is lower, during menopause and andropause.

THE CORTISOL CONNECTION

The stress hormone with the most significant physiological impact is cortisol, the hormone solicited during long-term stress. Cortisol, a glucocorticoid, is produced by the adrenal cortex during stress. Therefore, excessive cortisol production can impact hormones produced by this part of the adrenal glands. This also explains many of the long-term effects of stress on the body. Indeed, with continued stress the body begins to change its way of functioning to have detrimental and irreversible effects on health and well-being.

Cortisol functions to increase blood sugar through gluconeogenesis; suppress the immune system; and aid in fat, protein, and carbohydrate metabolism. Cortisol also inhibits bone formation. Though short-term stresses increase adrenalin production, long-term stress invariably has an effect on increasing cortisol production.

Researchers show that chronically elevated cortisol impedes the body's ability to shut down stress-related cortisol production, thereby maintaining a continued high level of cortisol even when the stress is quite normal. As we review effects of cortisol on the body, we'll begin to understand how this vicious cycle can produce a wide variety of debilitating symptoms through interactions with neurotransmitters, gastrointestinal and other organs, and hormone production.

CORTISOL AND NEUROTRANSMITTERS

Serotonin is a neurotransmitter involved in triggering and maintaining sleep, mood maintenance (antianxiety and antidepressant), appetite control, pain perception, and intestinal tract movement control (intestinal motility). Researchers have long known increased cortisol to actually cause a drop in serotonin levels, predisposing insomnia, anxiety, depression, increased perception of pain, and gastrointestinal problems.

This effect of cortisol on lowering serotonin would be a good thing in the context of a life-threatening situation. If you live in a village surrounded by enemies, it's a good thing not to sleep deeply so you can hear the enemy breaking through the gates. If you are fighting or fleeing, it's a good thing not to be too relaxed. It's better to have heightened awareness, even a certain level of anxiety to keep you on your toes. However, continually high levels of cortisol can have detrimental effects.

By measuring changes in cortisol and certain neurotransmitters, researchers have connected stress effects to severe chronic diseases including asthma, chronic active hepatitis, chronic relapsing hepatitis, Crohn's disease, multiple sclerosis, rheumatoid arthritis, systemic lupus erythematous, trigeminal neuralgia, and ulcerative colitis. The researchers concluded, "An uncoping stress mechanism underlies diseases of these patients." It is interesting to notice that many of the diseases evaluated are considered autoimmune diseases.

CORTISOL AND GASTROINTESTINAL HEALTH

Cortisol has been shown to have important effects on the gastro-intestinal tract, including those caused by decreased serotonin levels. Indeed, research has shown that cortisol can stimulate colonic transit and lower pain thresholds in the gastrointestinal tract. Think of the individuals who experience diarrhea or abdominal pain (or both) when stressed. When stressed, your body doesn't know you cannot fight or flee. It increases blood flow to the parts of the body most important to the fight or flight processes, depriving those parts that are less important or even detrimental to the escape. Of course, digestion is less important than muscle reactivity or mental alertness during these times.

Cortisol can also affect intestinal permeability, leading to what has been termed "leaky gut." When healthy, the intestinal mucosa limits or stops the absorption of useless or dangerous substances into the blood from the intestinal tract. This can include bacteria, yeast, parasites, intact proteins, and many foodborne chemicals. In fact, a healthy mucosa can facilitate or encourage the absorption of beneficial substances into the bloodstream, including vitamins, minerals, trace elements, and peptides. When this selective permeability is impaired, intestinal inflammation occurs. This, in turn, can lead to downstream health problems such as food allergies or sensitivities (also known as delayed hypersensitivity reactions).

CORTISOL AND THE ENDOCRINE GLANDS

Not surprisingly cortisol has several effects on both endocrine and exocrine glands. The endocrine glands, by the way, are the ones that secrete hormones into the bloodstream, while exocrine glands secrete hormones outside of the glands and in some cases even outside of the body. We'll review only a few of the effects of cortisol on the glands, though these are important in explaining many of the effects of stress on various symptoms.

CORTISOL AND THE LIVER

Blood sugar increases with stress. If not used for fight or flight, the liver must convert the sugar back into glycogen and stock it. Research has shown that chronically elevated cortisol and associated carbohydrate metabolism by the liver can overburden this organ. Indeed, research has associated elevated cortisol to hepatic steatosis (fatty liver), as well as to high cholesterol and triglycerides. This is how stress can lead to a fatty liver diagnosis for someone who has never consumed excess fat, cholesterol, or alcohol.

CORTISOL AND THE PANCREAS

Clonidine is a drug shown to successfully treat acute pancreatitis. Clonidine is also a drug that ultimately reduces cortisol levels. This strongly suggests that high levels of cortisol negatively affect the pancreas, especially as related to glucagon and insulin production. Of course, this not surprising given that one of the major roles of cortisol is to raise blood sugar.

CORTISOL AND REPRODUCTIVE HORMONES

Cortisol has a variety of hormonal effects. This is particularly evident in women, although men are certainly also affected. Research has shown that elevated cortisol reduces production of all reproductive hormones. One such cortisol effect is on progesterone production. Keep in mind that progesterone is the gestational (pro – gestation) or "pregnancy hormone."

Since cortisol and progesterone compete for common receptors in the cells, cortisol impairs progesterone activity, setting the stage for estrogen dominance. Chronically elevated cortisol levels can be a direct cause of estrogen dominance, with all the familiar PMS symptoms.

This can explain why some women have difficulty getting pregnant while under stress. My friends Janet and Paul desperately wanted children. Both were high-strung and very active professionals. Not having children was, according to them, the biggest stressor in their lives. After years of trying to get pregnant they decided that it was probably better to be childless. After all, they were getting on in years. Once they made this decision their stress levels dropped considerably. You can probably guess what happened next: a few months after letting go of the "obligation" to have a child, Janet was pregnant.

Our cells contain receptors modeled to receive specific chemicals, which, when interacting with the receptor, trigger specific reactions. It's just like a lock and key. You've probably had the experience of easily inserting a key into a lock, but it's a key that won't turn. It slid into the keyhole, but it's the wrong key. And while the wrong key is in the keyhole, you cannot use the correct one. As noted by Dr. John Lee, cortisol and progesterone compete for receptors in cells. When one binds to a receptor, the other cannot.

This can lead to an interesting and sometimes confusing situation. You might have normal levels of progesterone as confirmed by a blood test. However, because cortisol blocks progesterone from binding to its appropriate receptor sites, pregnancy cannot occur.

The competitive relationship of cortisol and progesterone often leads to problems of excess estrogen activity or "estrogen dominance." Estrogen and progesterone must balance each other, with progesterone reducing the effects of excess estrogen.

During stressful periods it is possible to have excess cortisol, low progesterone activity, and symptoms of excess estrogen. High levels of cortisol could therefore be an important, albeit overlooked cause of premenstrual symptoms. Another point needing mention: Cortisol may actually increase estrogen production. Dr. Natasha Turner describes this in an excellent consumer-oriented article in *Chatelaine* magazine. The competitive effects of cortisol and progesterone regarding menopausal symptoms have also been discussed in a variety of studies and in many excellent books. One has to wonder if this can explain why, in most cases, stress seems to affect women more significantly than it does men.

We can't end this section without a quick note about libido. A significant number of individuals attest to a libido drop during stress. Cortisol and the downstream hormonal effects may well be involved in this drop in sex drive. Dr. Melvyn Werbach expresses this in his characteristic fashion: "Engaging in reproductive behavior during escape is also counterproductive. Therefore, elevated cortisol suppresses the production of all major reproductive hormones."

CORTISOL AND THYROID FUNCTION

Stress can have a major effect on thyroid gland function. And vice versa. The relationship between the adrenal gland cortisol production and the thyroid glands is well established. There is a feedback mechanism between the two that is essential for survival. Our thyroid glands control metabolism. Stated simply, they control the speed at which a variety of functions take place in the body, including how we use up calories.

In hypothyroidism (low thyroid function) the body uses up fewer calories. Individuals with hypothyroidism may have difficulty losing weight even though they don't eat to excess and they exercise. Their bodies basically just burn fewer calories via a slowed metabolism.

For perspective, it's important to note that the thyroid gland itself mainly secretes the T4 thyroid hormone, along with small amounts of the other thyroid hormone, T3. About one third of the T4 is converted into T3, which is the more biologically active form. Cortisol has been shown to decrease the conversion of T4 to T3. So basically, you may have "normal" T4 levels, but with excess cortisol, the T4 might not correctly convert into the active T3 form.

To quote Dr. Werbach again, "This raises the question of whether hypothyroidism, a common disorder in our society, could be better treated by optimizing stress physiology than by hormone replacement."

Cortisol has been shown to have negative effects on many other hormone or hormone-like substances. Research has shown that excess cortisol is involved in DHEA, androgens, insulin-like growth hormone, and growth hormone imbalances. Insulin-like growth hormones, which are also called insulin-like growth factors, are proteins that are chemically very similar to insulin. Growth hormone, on the other hand, is produced in and secreted by the pituitary gland. It stimulates growth as well as cell reproduction and repair in humans. Both of these hormones act in different yet complementary ways. Growth hormone is necessary in order to stimulate the liver to produce insulin-like growth hormone. Once this is done, the insulin-like growth hormone stimulates growth or repair, especially in the muscles, cartilage, bones, and nerves. The negative impact of cortisol on insulin-like growth hormone may explain why stress can be so detrimental to muscle mass, joints, bones, and nerves.

If you suffer from a variety of symptoms associated with stress, if your blood tests seem to show that everything is fine, and if you've gone through a number of stressors (recall your Social Readjustment Rating Scale score) you may suffer from the insidious effects of stress on hormonal balance.

CORTISOL AND INSULIN RESISTANCE

We've already discussed the role of cortisol in increased blood sugar for fight or flight energy. This is how the impact of long-term stress or long-term overreaction to stress is related to metabolic syndrome, or Syndrome X.

Syndrome X also is known by a variety of other names. These include cardiometabolic syndrome, insulin resistance syndrome, and, in Australia, the highly appropriate CHAOS (coronary artery disease, hypertension, atherosclerosis, obesity, and stroke). The term syndrome denotes several clinically recognizable features or symptoms that often occur together. It is not a disease per se, but is used to describe a group of symptoms as they occur in an individual. We can also think of chronic fatigue syndrome, irritable bowel syndrome, and others.

In metabolic syndrome, symptoms include:

- Abdominal obesity (belly fat)
- High LDL cholesterol (bad cholesterol)
- Low HDL cholesterol (good)
- High triglycerides
- High blood pressure
- High blood sugar (type II diabetes)

Most develop these symptoms individually and gradually over months or sometimes years. This gradual development of metabolic syndrome is insidious. You start developing a little more belly fat, perhaps within normal limits; LDL cholesterol increases from one blood test to another, as may glucose and triglycerides. Everything seems OK until increases reach levels considered abnormal. When two or three values are above normal limits, risk for heart disease is very high.

There is very little doubt that stress, poor diet, and sedentary lifestyle are the three major pillars of metabolic syndrome. We are (I hope) taught about proper diet and encouraged to get active. Unfortunately, we are seldom informed about the dire importance of tired, burnt-out adrenal glands.

CHAPTER SIX

Stress, Cortisol, and the Gut

IN MANY CASES, ONGOING STRESS can result in major debilitating effects. Stress can affect a variety of systems not (seemingly) directly associated. It's not just digestion; it's digestion and hormones and sleep and concentration and cholesterol and weight gain and . . . well, you get the point. The digestion issues alone, however, can be a significant challenge for my patients.

Adrenal stress, along with the associated potential for elevated cortisol levels, often leads to digestive difficulties. Cortisol can affect bowel transit and intestinal permeability. This, in turn, can lead to the development of food intolerances, nutritional deficiencies, irritable bowel syndrome, fibromyalgia, and even anxiety disorders.

CORTISOL AND TYPE III FOOD ALLERGIES

It's important to make a distinction between food allergies and food intolerances.

Different types of reactions to specific foods are often called food allergies or intolerances. While these terms are often used interchangeably, they are distinctly different. True food allergies, also called Type I food allergies, trigger an immediate reaction and are characterized by the presence of a certain type of antibody known as IgE. These IgE antibodies can trigger an increase in inflammatory complexes called leukotrienes, as well as TNF-alpha, or tumor necrosis factor. The latter can also amplify the effects of cortisol and increase the risk of insulin resistance.

Food intolerance, on the other hand, occurs because the body lacks the digestive enzyme needed to digest the particular food. Common food intolerances include gluten intolerance and lactose intolerance.

Type III allergies (also referred to as food sensitivities) are very different from both Type I allergies and food intolerances. Like Type I allergies, they involve the production of antibodies. However, they solicit IgG antibodies, not IgE. Furthermore, this type of allergy can produce a delayed reaction—sometimes up to three days after eating the offending food. This makes it difficult to identify the culprit. In addition, if you suffer from Type III allergies, you may actually crave the foods you are sensitive to. Continually eating foods you are sensitive to can, over time, contribute to a "leaky gut." Yet leaky gut can also solicit the formation of IgG antibodies, thereby leading to or worsening Type III allergies. This can lead to a vicious, and often frustrating, cycle until the offending foods are identified and avoided.

For more than 20 years, clinicians have thought food intolerances to be involved in a variety of complaints. Well-documented involvements include the respiratory tract (rhinitis, sinusitis, and asthma); the digestive tract (bloating, cramps, nausea, constipation, diarrhea, irritable bowel, Crohn's disease, and celiac disease); the skin (eczema, dermatitis, acne, and psoriasis); the central nervous system (migraines, headaches, vertigo, attention deficit-hyperactivity disorder, and depression); arthritic and inflammatory conditions (arthritis, fibromyalgia, and recurrent cramps); metabolism (type II diabetes, fatigue, thyroid problems, weight gain, and obesity); and hypertension.

Of course, these disorders may be caused by other factors, including stress. However, food intolerances are often an unsuspected factor in their development. The body considers these types of foods as aggressors and tries to destroy them. Unfortunately, the mechanisms the body uses are mechanisms that also harm our healthy cells. Inflammation and free radicals increase and cause damage to healthy cells in the process.

Because stress can lead to the development of delayed food reactions, or Type III allergies, identifying and eliminating the offending food is of utmost importance.

CORTISOL AND NUTRITIONAL DEFICIENCIES

Continued stress and/or high levels of cortisol can cause important nutrient deficiencies. I will address depletions in more detail in later chapters, but I want to highlight that many symptoms associated with stress may involve the loss of these nutrients. Therefore, when dealing with stress it is important to recognize that nutritional deficiencies have probably developed. Of course, these must be corrected for symptom improvement.

You've probably heard "you are what you eat." This is only partly true. You are a product of what you eat, digest, and absorb, what you don't eliminate, and what you waste uselessly. Stress causes a loss of nutrients, vitamins, minerals, fatty acids, and amino acids. As mentioned earlier, a loss of any number of these can also account for symptoms associated with stress.

The table on the next page lists nutrients commonly depleted during stress.

NUTRIENT	EFFECTS OF DEPLETION	WHY
MAGNESIUM	Signs of deficiency include asthma, muscle cramps (especially at night or after physical exertion), arrhythmias, insomnia, gastrointestinal disorders, kidney stones, osteoporosis, anxiety, depression, fatigue, headaches or migraines, PMS, high blood pressure, and high cholesterol.	Because it is involved in relaxing muscles and nerves as well as reducing acidity in the body, magnesium is probably the most depleted nutrient in periods of stress.
POTASSIUM	Signs of deficiency include irregular heartbeat, poor reflexes, muscle weakness, fatigue, thirst, water retention, constipation, dizziness, and nervous disorders.	Stress increases the release of mineralocorticoids by the adrenal glands. These, in turn, cause an accrued loss of potassium and greater than normal sodium retention.
VITAMIN B5	Signs of deficiency include fatigue, dermatitis, burning feet and/or hands, numbness in the extremities, muscle cramps, tingling sensations, irritability, fatigue, tiredness, and impaired alcohol detoxification.	Vitamin B5, or pantothenic acid, is necessary for steroid hormone production and adrenal gland function. It also improves stress reactions in otherwise healthy individuals.

Vitamin C	Deficiency symptoms include capillary fragility and easy bruising, gums that bleed easily, poor wound healing, poor appetite and growth, osteoporosis, skin problems, tender and swollen joints, and frequent infections	Vitamin C helps the body handle all types of stress. Stressful situations (both physical and emotional) deplete reserves of this vitamin quickly because it is required for the synthesis of the body's main stress hormones, including adrenaline and cortisol.
Tyrosine	Deficiency symptoms include depression, hypothyroidism, low blood pressure, restless leg syndrome, and vitiligo.	Tyrosine is involved in the production of thyroxin, the thyroid hormone, as well as the production of adrenalin and many neurotransmitters.
Zinc	Deficiency symptoms include acne; alopecia; impaired sense of smell and taste; delayed wound healing; decreased immunity (frequent infections); infertility; depression; photophobia; night blindness; problems with skin, hair, and nails; menstrual problems; and joint pain.	Cortisol increases urinary excretion of zinc.

FIBROMYALGIA, IRRITABLE BOWEL SYNDROME, AND ANXIETY DISORDERS

Both fibromyalgia and irritable bowel syndrome (IBS) are diagnoses of exclusion. That means the diagnosis itself is a description of the symptoms, without any clear indicator of why the symptoms exist.

Anxiety disorder, or "nervousness," as it has been called in the past, is a similar kind of diagnosis. The category includes generalized anxiety disorder (GAD), obsessive-compulsive disorder (OCD), panic disorder, post-traumatic stress disorder (PTSD), and social phobia (or social anxiety disorder). There is an important increase in this category of symptoms, including the PTSD. Of course, the reasons are not only physiological; they are also social and spiritual.

A fibromyalgia diagnostic indicator is pain in at least half of 18 trigger points. This pain is not essentially inflammatory; indeed, if we see inflammation it is often a side effect, not a cause. Any inflammation is marked with the suffix "itis," such as arthritis or gastritis.

The word fibromyalgia includes "algia," the suffix that means "pain." When we say someone has fibromyalgia, we're basically saying his or her muscle (myo) fibers (fibro) hurt (algia). Patients with fibromyalgia have pain, but there doesn't seem to be a reason for the pain. Furthermore, fibromyalgia is often characterized by other symptoms as well. Patients often experience problems with sleep and depression. In most cases, researchers admit that symptoms sometimes begin after a physical trauma, surgery, infection, or significant psychological stress.

PUTTING THE PIECES TOGETHER

Recall that cortisol can reduce serotonin levels. As we know, serotonin is important for proper sleep, as an antidepressant, and as an anxiety reducer. It's critical for this discussion that we remember that serotonin functions to reduce the perception of pain.

If your serotonin levels are low, you could have an accrued perception of pain and would feel more pain than reasonable for any given situation. Reduced serotonin would also cause problems with sleep and depression. Furthermore, if stress were the cause of the problem, not only would your serotonin levels be low, but you would also have low levels of magnesium, increasing the chance for muscle pain, depression, and insomnia.

Fibromyalgia is most often an effect, not a cause. My clinical work over two decades confirms this. Of course, stress is most often a trigger. However, each symptom can increase others. Continual muscle pain and poor sleep, along with uncertainty about the causes of both, can lead to depression as an effect of the entire chain.

A FIBROMYALGIA STORY

Rachel was diagnosed with fibromyalgia in the mid-1980s. Rachel's fibromyalgia seemed to have been triggered by a car accident. After this stressful event nothing seemed the same. Rachel had terrible problems sleeping and her muscles and joints ached with no signs of inflammation.

Continued pain and sleeplessness caused difficulty in accomplishing daily tasks. Everything seemed increasingly difficult. Since repeated blood tests and her frequent physical exams gave no indication of any physical health problem, Rachel was told she was "simply depressed." Though she never gave any serious thought to ending her life, Rachel felt she was increasingly becoming a burden to her friends and family. The situation was dire.

I recommended a nutritional protocol to alleviate the effects of stress and repair what was damaged, as well as to ensure that future stressors would not affect her body. We checked for food intolerances and nutritional deficiencies and adjusted her diet accordingly.

Within a few weeks Rachel was sleeping more soundly than she had in years. Her energy level increased proportionately to her improved sleep. Her pain gradually subsided and only returned when she "cheated" on her new and healthy diet. She is now "the Rachel everyone knew before the accident."

AN IRRITABLE BOWEL SYNDROME STORY

Each year, I see hundreds of patients with non-specific gastrointestinal disorder. This condition is called irritable bowel when tests cannot detect any abnormality but one or more of the following symptoms are present: cramps, abdominal pain, bloating, gas, diarrhea, and constipation.

Claudia was diagnosed with irritable bowel syndrome at age 23. A medical student with excellent grades, she suffered from gas, bloating, and diarrhea. The gas and bloating were "tolerable," but the diarrhea was not. She could have three or four episodes a day often with no warning and always with a sense of urgency. Her symptoms had begun her first year of college and increased in both intensity and frequency by the time she came to my office. Claudia had reached the point where she would always inquire as to the availability of washrooms wherever she went. On occasion she even wore adult diapers, "just in case!"

The gas, bloating, and diarrhea were ruining Claudia's academic and social life. The situation became worst, psychologically at least, when an endoscopy, a colonoscopy, and celiac disease test came up negative. Of course, since stress made the symptoms worse and the diarrhea more frequent, Claudia was told she needed to rest and was prescribed an antidepressant.

Fortunately, Claudia's mother had read my book on candida and suggested that Claudia consider the possibility of candida or yeast infection. Claudia had taken significant amounts of antibiotics for her persistent acne.

Though candida did not, in fact, play a role in Claudia's symptoms, we discovered she had developed many symptoms consistent with a deficiency of vitamin B3. Deficiency of vitamin B3, or niacin, can cause what has been termed the "3 Ds," diarrhea, depression (or dementia in older persons), and dermatitis.

Claudia certainly had the diarrhea and she also had the dermatitis. We also found that Claudia, a sugarholic, was significantly affected by her excessive sugar consumption. Finally, a test revealed severe intolerance to wheat, even though the celiac test had not been conclusive.

Claudia cut out wheat and followed a nutritional program to reduce sugar cravings. This made sugar withdrawal less difficult and she was able to increase her vitamin B3 intake and balance out a few other deficient minerals. Within days off the wheat, the diarrhea was almost completely gone and Claudia's skin had actually improved.

Stress had triggered a variety of reactions and caused nutritional deficiencies, both of which needed to be reversed. These stressors included the academic demands that were made on her as a medical student, as well as severe nutritional deficiencies brought on by a particularly bad diet. I believed, and still believe, that Claudia went through a very intense stress as a child or adolescent. When I suggested this might be the case, she became very uncomfortable and changed the subject. This stress, if it happened, may have played a role in weakening her adrenal glands, but we may never know. Claudia is now symptom free, only two months after starting her new nutritional program. When she cheats, and she does occasionally, she knows what to expect. Claudia's symptoms were triggered by stress.

AN ANXIETY DISORDER STORY

The symptoms of anxiety disorders are basically those of an abnormal or disproportionate reaction to stress. Anxiety is a normal reaction to stress and can actually be beneficial in some situations. For some people, however, anxiety can become excessive. While the person suffering may realize their anxiety is too much, they may also have difficulty controlling it and it may negatively affect their day-to-day living.

Alex was pastor of a small congregation in the southwest. A typical intellectual (I might even say a nerd), he was loved by his congregation for his wisdom, as well as his patience. His neighbors delighted in his wit and his wife agreed on all counts.

Most did not know this godly man was fighting the demons of anxiety. Alex was restless. His sleep was punctuated with periods of anxiety and he often was awoken in a panic by his rushing heartbeat. He was even feeling less empathy for his congregants. Alex was increasingly unable to bear what his congregation and his friends asked him to deal with.

He was able to understand the needs presented to him, but he overreacted. When he was confronted with the problems of a couple in marital distress, had to comfort a bereaved church member, or had to prepare a sermon, he could feel his face flush, his heart began to rush, and he knew his sleep would be hectic.

His doctor told him that he had high blood pressure and arrhythmia. Alex didn't want to take medication unless it was absolutely necessary. Besides, he wanted to find out why he was reacting, not just cover the symptoms. A member of Alex's congregation offered to pay for a consultation with me.

As I chatted with Alex I realized that this man was in effect burning the candle at both ends. He hadn't taken a real vacation in over 10 years, and his diet was horrible. In addition, Alex and his wife had wanted children. However, both were infertile and Alex's meager wages did not permit fertility treatments or adoption.

I explained to Alex his problems were physiological, not psychological. The fact that he tried to control himself in front of members of his congregation, which he did quite successfully so far, demonstrated that his psyche was just fine. So, the physician was right in suggesting medication. However, the medication and the diagnosis did not tell us why Alex had these symptoms or how he could reduce or avoid the use of medication. My objective was to help Alex understand the effects of stress on his body so he could make the appropriate nutritional and lifestyle changes to correct the problem and eliminate the symptoms.

Think about it: If, like Alex, you're conscious enough to recognize your reaction as abnormal and in control enough to try to reduce the reaction, your psychological state is fine.

The "psychological" overreaction is often just the body—or more specifically your adrenal glands—overreacting to stress. While psychological factors do indeed play an important role in the stress response, the physical factors, which are at least as important, are frequently overlooked. I explained to Alex that his reactions, wakefulness, rapid heartbeat, and muscle tension would all be normal if he was in fact in danger. The problem is not his reaction per se, but instead the fact that he is over-reacting at all.

Before a burnout, when the adrenal glands have been overtired, they often begin to overreact to stress. This overreaction to normal stressors is often described as anxiety or panic attacks. This was Alex's problem; he was suffering from what Dr. James Wilson has appropriately termed "adrenal fatigue."

I convinced Alex he had to take a real vacation. I asked him to take "off time," remembering the admonition of the psalmist, "Be still, and know that I am God." We improved his diet so that his adrenal glands were "fed" properly, and we agreed that he should tell the members of his congregation what was happening so they would not place unnecessary demands on his time.

Alex improved quickly; the very fact that he understood why he was overreacting was already reducing his stress. His sleep and energy both improved. Six months later, the change was noticeable. Alex had had no idea stress could cause so much physiological damage. He told me that his own experience was helping him understand others.

CHAPTER SEVEN

Rules to Remember About Stress Adaptation

THE CONTENT IN THIS CHAPTER, although short, may be the key to help you reduce the effects of past stress and prime your body so that future stresses will not be as damaging. As with anything, dealing with stress requires that we respect certain rules of biology. Each rule on the next page will help in general and will also make each element of my stress plan easier to follow.

RULE #1: UNDERSTAND THE STRESS PROCESS

1. Stress is anything that causes the body or the mind to change what they are used to. Stress can be emotional, environmental, hormonal, immune, physical, or psychological.
2. The body reacts the same way to any change or stress, whether it "seems" good or bad.
3. When stressed, the body prepares itself to fight or flee. It increases any function that can help in the fight or flight process and it reduces any function that is not necessary to fight or flight.
4. Today we can neither fight nor flee in most cases where the fight or flight response is solicited.
5. The impact of stress on the body is cumulative, like the proverbial drop that makes the bucket overflow or the straw that breaks the camel's back.

6. The cumulative impact of stress is insidious. As stress increases, the body changes, nutritional deficiencies develop, certain glands begin to change the way they operate, certain activities that are important during stress continue to operate even when there is little or no stress.
7. The impact of stress is primarily biochemical and physiological.

RULE #2: REMEMBER PASCAL

Blaise Pascal was a 17th century mathematician, physicist, and philosopher. Though he is remembered for his scientific discoveries, his philosophical works have had a much more lasting effect on our culture.

Pascal wrote, *"Qui essaie de faire l'ange fini toujours par faire la bête."* Translation: The person who tries to act like an angel generally ends up acting like a beast. The point of Pascal's comment is that we are not disincarnated. We cannot, indeed should not, try to act like angels.

A patient of mine woke up the day following our initial consultation. She knew that the accumulated stress was a major factor in her life and she knew what the continued stressors were. So, the first thing she did was to call up her boss to resign. The second was to tell her boyfriend/roommate to leave. Now neither of these decisions was wrong per se; her boss never respected her talents and abused her time and energy. Her boyfriend, who was also her roommate, brought nothing constructive to their relationship and took a significant amount of her time and energy. In making these changes, she was trying to help decrease her levels of stress.

Here's the problem: In quitting her job, she lost her salary. In losing her salary, she created a new stress—no money. She could live on her savings, but she now had to find a new job, and that too is a stress. She hadn't eliminated stress; she had just changed its face. As far as her roommate was concerned, although he was a useless idiot (her terms, not mine) he did pay part of the rent. So, not only was she now jobless, but she also owed twice as much rent each month. By trying to eliminate stress, she created incredible new stress.

Many individuals, when they realize the impact of stress on their lives, want to eliminate it all. They want to throw away the baby, the bath water, and the bath as well. This, however, can be stressful. So, before you decide to eliminate everything that stresses you, ask yourself about what new stresses you might be courting.

Takeaway: Do what you can, change what you must, don't go crazy, and don't use what you've just read as an excuse to do too little.

RULE #3: REMEMBER THE CHAIR

Stress, like any health problem, is multifactorial. Analogically, we could compare stress and the tools to deal with it to a chair. The seat of your chair is made up of your genetics and other unchangeable characteristics. The chair, however, has four legs, all of which can influence the state of your stress glands. One leg of the chair is exercise, a second leg is rest, one leg is made up of the psycho-spiritual aspects, and one leg is nutrition. Now what happens as you are seated on the chair if one of your chair's legs is shorter or longer than another?

When dealing with stress we must address all the factors involved. We may be able to change some things quickly, but others will take more time. That's all right, as long as all the legs are balanced before we fall off of the chair! The complete process may be lengthy, but it must be undertaken until it is complete. For some, it is a lifelong endeavor; there is that much to change. Remember, it's fine as long as you begin the process.

RULE #4: EAT BETTER

Nutrition can be your most valuable ally. The foods we eat have significant effects on our stress levels, as well as on our adrenals. Though there are many stressors we cannot control immediately, and others we will never be able to control, we can control how and what we eat. Good nutrition is critical to effective stress management.

RULE #5: START STRESS ADAPTATION NOW

Most of us find excuses to procrastinate. Stress does not wait or stop, and effects are cumulative. You are the only one to make the changes to manage stress. Start now.

The next chapters each contain a section "Simple Changes to Make NOW." These sections offer simple, immediately applicable, and inexpensive changes you should adopt straightaway to help you deal with stress and its negative effects.

CHAPTER EIGHT

Key Nutritional Elements for Stress

WHEN I LECTURE TO HIGH SCHOOL STUDENTS I enjoy asking them, "What is the most intimate thing you do?" Invariably, I'll hear giggles from my audience. They realize that I don't mean what they're thinking when I tell them, "It's eating! What can be more intimate than your relationship with what you eat? After all, what you ingest becomes you!" Think about it, every bit of your body—brain cells, neurotransmitters, hormones, antibodies, bones, skin, and the cells of your digestive, respiratory and genito-urinary tracts—are made from what you eat.

These nutrients play three roles in the body. Nutrients like proteins, fats, and carbohydrates serve as a source of energy. Nutrients also make up the building blocks, or "plastics," for our cells. This is the role of proteins, certain fats, and certain minerals. Finally, particular nutrients act as catalysts and are needed to trigger the speeding, slowing, or stopping of various reactions in the body. Catalyst nutrients include amino acids, vitamins, minerals, and trace elements.

Each nutritional role is absolutely critical. Even so, most nutrition education and conversation tends to limit focus on catalyst nutrients. A car metaphor is helpful here. Gas would be your source of energy. Metal and rubber would be your plastic, building block elements. The spark plugs would be catalysts. Without all three of these working properly, your car isn't moving.

This is why it's so important to avoid refined foods in favor of whole and unrefined choices. Whole grains pack the calories (fuel) and the proteins, along with the catalyst workforce required to properly metabolize them. When eating a refined food, your body has to dig into reserves of nutrients that could be needed elsewhere in the body. Refined sugar food choices are especially poor choices when dealing with stress.

THE "SUGAR BLUES"

Few foods are as synonymous with relaxation as sugary foods or alcoholic beverages. Alcohol is essentially super-refined sugar. Sugary foods send a message to the brain indicating pleasure. This response may be due to preferences for energy-dense sweet and high-fat foods that developed for reasons of survival. Indeed, sugar is demanded by the body during the fight or flight response.

The majority of the sugar consumed by Americans is refined. It packs the calories and taste, but lacks nutrients the body needs to use it effectively. Eating refined sugar actually depletes nutrients vital for a healthy stress response. These include vitamin B3 (niacin), vitamin B5, vitamin B6, chromium, magnesium, and zinc.

Vitamin B5 is required for carbohydrate metabolism. That means the more sugar you consume, the more B5 you require. When you consume a refined carbohydrate, because it doesn't have B5, your body must use the B5 that it would have used for some other function. Because vitamin B5 is required for the proper functioning of the adrenal glands, refined carbohydrate consumption and the resulting B5 depletion can inhibit adrenal function.

Refined sugars also have a negative effect on blood sugar balance. Overconsumption of refined sugars and refined carbohydrates (white bread, white rice, etc.) stimulates the pancreas to produce excessive insulin. Over time, this overproduction of insulin lowers blood sugar. At this point, the adrenal glands must work to bring blood sugar levels back to balance. The pancreas and adrenals are both overworked in this scenario.

A SAD SUGAR STORY

Nicholas is an intelligent, some would say brilliant, 8-year-old. Unfortunately, Nick has been diagnosed with an attention deficit-hyperactivity disorder. And, like many children, Nicholas was prescribed Ritalin. If we look at the poor child's diet, one thing becomes evident. Nick is fueled with excessive amounts of sugar for breakfast. Nicholas loves one of the most popular breakfast cereals, one that packs almost 50 percent sugar. Yes, you read that right. So Nicholas consumes an obscene amount of sugar around 8 a.m. Around 10 a.m. his blood sugar drops and his adrenal glands react to maintain the blood sugar at normal levels. As the adrenals react, Nicholas is inundated with stress hormones. He become fidgety, he has difficulty concentrating, and his whole body is primed to fight or flee. Of course he can't concentrate on what the teacher is saying!

For lunch, things improve somewhat. Nicholas gets a whitebread sandwich with prepared meats and a fruit drink that contains 10 percent natural juice. Sugar, sugar, sugar, and more sugar. Of course Nicholas is hyperactive! His diet is loaded with excess sugar and deficient in protein, as well as most essential nutrients. Nicholas is probably eating more sugar than your average lumberjack 100 years ago, yet he's asked to stay still, not move, and listen attentively.

One hundred years ago Americans consumed 30 pounds or less of sugar per person per year. Note that this is also a period in time characterized by five to 10 times higher activity levels when compared to current averages. Americans now consume about 100 pounds of sugar per person per year. That translates to about 30 teaspoons a day! Other sources give significantly higher levels of consumption. According to Linda Tarr Kent, author of the article "What Diseases Come From Eating Too Much Sugar," "Per capita sugar consumption in 2010 was almost 132 lbs. That compares to ... about 12 lbs. in the early 1800s."

The trend chart below compares increased sugar consumption against decreased level of physical activity. Obviously, both values are going in the wrong direction, and each complicates the other.

SUGAR CONSUMPTION VS PHYSICAL ACTIVITY

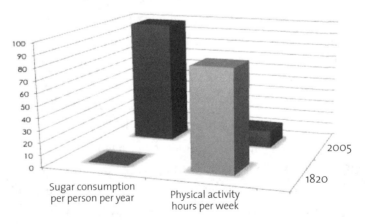

Bear in mind that these values include all sugars from all food sources, not just the teaspoon of white sugar you add to your coffee or the sugar in your can of pop. You would be surprised to learn about the sugar amounts in many "non-sugared" foods.

This table highlights the amount of "hidden" sugar in a typical and seemingly healthy diet.

FOOD	SUGAR Teaspoon equivalent
BREAKFAST	
Orange juice – 1 cup	7
Raisin Bran cereal – 1 cup	5
Low-fat milk – ½ cup	1
MID MORNING SNACK	
Blueberry yogurt – 1 cup	6
LUNCH	
Apple juice – 1 cup	10
Cheese sandwich	1
Peach – 1 medium	2
MID AFTERNOON SNACK	
Frozen yogurt smoothie	13
DINNER	
Pizza – 1 slice	1
Vanilla almond milk	3
Romaine lettuce with salad dressing	2
TOTAL	**51**

The following list of "bad choices" and "better choices" includes sweetener types by refinement and glycemic index (GI). The glycemic index number represents how fast the sugar enters the bloodstream. The lower the GI, the better the choice. What I term "bad" sugars are those with the highest GI and greatest negative impact on your adrenal glands and capacity to adapt to stress. These are the types you should try to avoid as much as possible.

The "better" sugars cause less damage and far less nutritional stress on the body. However, an excess of any type of sugar is detrimental to health. Our increased sugar consumption doesn't only affect our ability to handle stress, it also increases our risk of obesity, cardiovascular disease, and diabetes. New research is also suggesting that sugar may have the same effects as alcohol on the liver.

BAD CHOICES: Caramel, corn syrup, dextrose, fructose, galactose, glucose, golden syrup, high fructose corn syrup, inverted sugar, lactose, maltodextrin, maltose, refiner's syrup, sucrose, and trehalose.

BETTER CHOICES: Barley malt syrup, blackstrap molasses, brown rice syrup, coconut palm sugar, honey, maltitol, maple syrup, raw cane juice, and xylitol.

Stress itself affects the body's blood sugar–regulating mechanisms. "The efficiency of the adrenal cortex, which produces the adrenalin, may eventually be reduced, owing to its continual excitation from prolonged stress, and thus sufficient adrenalin may not be produced to raise the blood sugar when needed. The net result of all this is a defective stress mechanism coupled with hypoglycemia," wrote Carl Pfeiffer in the booklet *Mental and Elemental Nutrients.*

My first and most important nutritional recommendation is to cut down on refined carbohydrates, which include the sugars on the "bad choices" list, refined flour, and white rice products. If you do eat something sweet, try to eat it with protein in order to reduce its effect on blood sugar. The consumption of protein with carbs is recommended for a variety of reasons. First, if you eat protein with your carbohydrates, you'll feel full faster and eat fewer carbs. Second, the experience of a significant number of health professionals suggests that consuming protein along with carbohydrates reduces the speed at which latter is absorbed into the bloodstream. This helps reduce the spike in blood sugar that is then followed by a rapid drop. When blood sugar drops too much, the adrenal glands must intervene to help maintain blood glucose levels. This then stresses the adrenals.

PROTEIN: NOT JUST FOR MUSCLE HEADS

The Greek root meaning of the word protein is "that which comes first." Indeed, the difference between inanimate objects like stones and animate ones like plants or humans is the presence of protein.

Proteins provide our source of amino acids, an important nutritional category. All neurotransmitters, enzymes, hormones, and antibodies are made of amino acids. Our bones are also made up of amino acids; calcium is only about 15 to 18 percent of the dry weight of our bones! Amino acids also make up our skin proteins (collagen and elastin) and our cartilage.

Proteins are a major source of energy, and protein-based tissue is continually used up for energy during stressful periods and when blood sugar is too low. This is referred to as gluconeogenesis (GNG). GNG is a metabolic pathway that results in the production of glucose from non-carbohydrate carbon substrates such as amino acids. When the body needs to generate "new" glucose it can break down its own protein-based tissues to use them as a source of energy. The phenomenon has been termed "auto-cannibalism." In this instance, the body causes short-term damage in order to ensure long-term survival.

So yes, proteins are very important, and no, we may not be getting enough. As I mentioned in the first part of this chapter, our sugar intake has increased alarmingly, passing from about 30 to 100 pounds per person per year. What's worse, this sugar increase has not corresponded with a necessary protein or physical activity increase.

Where can we get more protein? Concentrated protein sources include dairy, eggs, fish, legumes (beans), meats, nuts, poultry, and seeds, as well as shellfish. Eggs and beans are an excellent and inexpensive source of protein.

Sufficient protein consumption helps compensate for stress-based tissue damage and blood sugar imbalances. One recent study showed protein supplementation to improve the response to sugar in healthy individuals. Another demonstrated that a modest increase in protein content along with a reduction in consumption of high GI foods led to an improvement in weight loss.

According to most statistics, adults in the United States should get 10 to 35 percent of daily calories from protein foods. For stress situations, I suggest targeting the upper level. That's about 46 grams per day of protein for women and 56 grams for men. That may seem like a lot, but it's not. Just eight ounces of animal protein provides 28 grams of protein. A small portion of mixed nuts provides seven grams, and one egg or a few tablespoons of peanut butter provide another six grams. With some care, we can easily consume the right amount of protein to help manage the effects of stress.

PROTEIN CONTENT OF COMMON FOODS

FOOD	QUANTITY	PROTEIN (IN GRAMS)
Meat, poultry, or fish	30 g (1 oz.)	7
Whole egg	1 large	6
Dried peas or beans	125 ml (1/2 cup)	7
Cheese (cheddar), low-fat	30 g (1 oz.)	7
Firm tofu	85 ml (1/3 cup)	7
Mixed nuts	60 ml (1/4 cup)	7
Peanut butter (unsweetened)	15 ml (1 Tbsp.)	4

THE IMPORTANCE OF ACID-ALKALINE BALANCE

You may have heard that excess protein intake is harmful. Indeed, protein is acidic and acid-promoting. Excess protein intake has been associated with arthritis, sleep problems, increased risk of kidney stones, and a variety of other disorders. What is so dangerous about excess acid and why is the acid alkaline balance so important?

All liquids have a certain degree of acidity or alkalinity, measured by hydrogen potential (pH). The pH scale values range from 0 to 14, where "0" is extremely acidic, "14" extremely alkaline, and "7" is neutral—neither acid nor alkaline.

THE pH SCALE

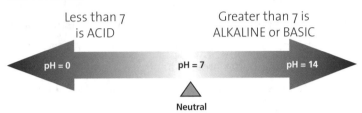

The pH of our cells is as important as the pH of our blood. Anyone who has worked with swimming pool chemicals knows that small changes in pH can cause important problems. All good bakers know that a change in the pH of a recipe significantly changes the end results.

Yes, our bodies are just like cupcakes! Any imbalance in our pH impacts physiological chemical reactions that give us energy, help us repair cells, or help us adapt to stress. The chemical reactions required to sustain life, produce energy, and encourage repair are all dependent on a proper cell pH. For optimal function, we want to maintain a slightly alkaline pH.

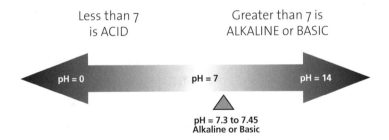

Our current lifestyles tend to push our bodies toward acidity. The worst culprits include too little (or too much) exercise, an acidifying diet, stress, and certain nutritional deficiencies, such as calcium, magnesium, potassium, and manganese. Just getting older can also make your body more acidic.

When our bodies become too acidic, a variety of symptoms gradually develop. In many cases, we blame these symptoms on "getting older." While increased age is indeed a factor in this phenomenon, acidosis is generally a controllable health element. When it comes to stress, it's hard to determine if acidosis is cause or effect. However, stress increases a variety of functions, whilst decreasing others. When we are stressed, the kidneys retain sodium but eliminate potassium, calcium, and magnesium. Even though sodium is an alkalinizing mineral, the loss of the other three increases the risk of acidity. Cortisol is also acidifying, which means that a frequent increase in cortisol can cause the body to become more acidic. What's more, the increase in the breakdown of protein-based tissues increases the amount of uric acid, thereby making the body more acidic. Overall, stress increases the body's acidic load in ways that are highly measurable.

An acidic body is a "stressed" body. One of the factors that cause most acidification in the body, apart from nutrition, is stress. The term subclinical acidosis is used to describe this type of excess acidity in cells.

WHAT CAUSES ACIDOSIS?

GENETIC PREDISPOSITION

In the 1980s French researcher Jean-Georges Henrotte discovered that the body's capacity to retain magnesium is in part genetic. His study, presented at the U.S. National Academy of Sciences, noted genetic variables affecting magnesium retention in some individuals.

As it happens, magnesium is one of the most critical buffering (acidity reducing) minerals in the body. Research has shown a direct link between magnesium levels in the body and our "stressability." Magnesium deficiency significantly increases our stressability. Therefore, subgroups of the population might be at risk of being both more easily stressed and also more easily acidic because of their genetic predisposition for magnesium retention.

STRESS

Stress decreases the pH to a more acidic environment in variety of ways. Cortisol increases the urinary loss of calcium, magnesium, and potassium, the body's most important alkalinizing minerals. Cortisol also increases stomach acid (HCl) thereby explaining the heartburn or ulcers that can develop during stress.

HORMONE LEVELS

Certain hormonal imbalances may increase magnesium loss and increase the risk of subclinical acidosis. Though normal levels of estrogen actually improve magnesium utilization, excess estrogen has actually been shown to hamper magnesium metabolism. Some contraceptives have an even greater effect in lowering magnesium levels.

EXCESSIVE EXERCISE

Exercise can help improve our pH by improving circulation (both vascular and lymphatic) and oxygenation. Excess exercise, however, can increase the risk of subclinical acidosis in two ways. Excess exercise, as with any stress, can lead to acid buildup in body tissues. Furthermore, once past the lactate threshold, lactic acid can accumulate in the blood and muscles.

IMBALANCED DIET

We can't overemphasize the importance of diet when addressing acid-alkaline balance. Every food has an acidic, alkaline, or neutral value. This value comes from the variety of substances that make up the food. The amount and ratio of vitamins, minerals, trace elements, fatty acids, and amino acids all influence acid or alkaline residue after consumption.

Surprisingly, foods that may taste acidic are not always those that leave acid residue after digestion and absorption. German researcher Dr. Thomas Remer developed a way to evaluate the relative acidity or alkalinity of the foods we eat. Potential renal acid load (PRAL) measures body acid load by measuring the amount of acid secreted by the kidneys. PRAL is expressed in milliequivalents (mEq). The higher the milliequivalent of a food, the greater the acid load on the body.

Researchers such as Remer have also begun to document the very negative effects of high PRAL foods on the general health of both children and adults. This research from the *Journal of the American Dietetics Association* is a good resource for review.

Another researcher, Dr. Anthony Sebastian compared the PRAL of our distant ancestors with ours. Sebastian found that we have gone from a –88 mEq per day to an average of +48 mEq today, a 60-point increase! Remember that the higher the mEq of a food, the greater the acid load on the body. At –88 mEq our ancestors had a VERY alkaline diet, at an average of +48 we have a VERY acidic diet.

Many researchers speculate that our increased acid load is a major factor in the increase of degenerative diseases in today's society. This of course also has a major role to play in increasing our body's reaction to stress, as well as decreasing its capacity to recuperate from very intense acute or prolonged chronic stresses.

IMPORTANT NOTES ON
THE ACID/ALKALINE BALANCE

1. You can't (and shouldn't) eliminate all acid-forming foods. You can, however, ensure a proper balance between these and the alkalinizing foods. This balance varies depending on the source you read. My recommendation is a ratio of 60 percent alkalinizing foods to 40 percent acidifying foods. Never have a diet that exceeds 50 percent acidifying foods.

2. Alkalinizing food should be predominant in our diets. The alkalinizing potential of any food, particularly fruits, depends on growing soil, the type of fertilizer used (compost versus standard fertilizer), and ripeness at the time of harvest.

3. One simple way to ensure an alkaline diet is to make sure both lunch and dinner consist of mostly vegetables, with 25 percent protein.

4. Quick fix: Eliminate overtly acidic foods such as sodas and fruit beverages. These offer little or no nutritional value and contain a lot of empty calories.

If you are like most and eat a Standard American Diet (SAD), your diet is far more acid-forming than alkalinizing. It is no surprise we see so many degenerative diseases! Changing the ratio, however, is not difficult. For breakfast, enjoy the eggs, meat, and fruits with just one slice of bread. For lunch or dinner, forego the bread entirely, cut your starch by half, and double your greens.

Balancing your acid/alkaline ratio is especially critical when you are challenged with the effects of stress. The following table provides a simple list of acid-forming or alkaline foods. You can use this information to make the healthiest nutrition choices to support health and stress management.

ALKALINE / ALKALINE FOOD CHART

ALKALINE	ACID-FORMING	NEUTRAL	VARIABLE
CEREAL GRAINS (used in the making of breakfast cereals, noodles and pasta, breads, cookies, pies, bagels, etc.)			
Millet and sprouted cereal grains	All cereal grains except millet (buckwheat, corn, oats, brown rice, spelt, kamut, white rice, rye, whole wheat, white flour, enriched flour) and everything made with these	Wild rice	
VEGETABLES These include aromatic herbs and spices			
All vegetables except potatoes and tomatoes			Potatoes and tomatoes may be acid-forming or alkaline depending on the type and the soil conditions. In the case of tomatoes it also depends on whether they have been vine-ripened or not.
FRUITS			
All fruits except cranberries, grapefruits, lemons, limes, and oranges that have not been tree-ripened	Cranberries; strawberries when not picked ripe		Grapefruits, lemons, limes, and oranges; strawberries, depending on when they were picked

ALKALINE	ACID-FORMING	NEUTRAL	VARIABLE
NUTS			
Almonds and chestnuts	All nuts except almonds and chestnuts		
SEEDS			
Sprouted seeds and pumpkin seeds	All seeds, including quinoa, except sprouted seeds and pumpkin seeds		
LEGUMES (Beans)			
Fermented or sprouted soya products	All legumes, including peanuts and non-fermented soya		
DAIRY			
Certain high-quality, organic, fermented yogurts and kefir, and low-fat cottage cheese; goat's whey	All higher-fat dairy products and all "processed" dairy products made with milk solids and milk by-products	All non-processed, low-fat dairy products	Whey protein, depending on the quality of the protein used and the manufacturing process, may be acid-forming, neutral, or lightly alkaline.
FISH			
	All fish		
SEAFOOD and SHELLFISH			
	All seafood and shellfish		

Alkaline	**Acid-forming**	**Neutral**	**Variable**
EGGS			
	Regular eggs	Free-range, organically fed chicken eggs	
POULTRY			
	Chicken, duck, grouse, turkey		
MEATS			
	Beef, bison, lamb, sheep, pork, rabbit, wild game		
BEVERAGES			
Vegetable juices, with the exception of some commercial products containing tomato juice; fresh fruit juices; green tea; water	Coffee, soft drinks (pop); all alcoholic beverages (beer, wine, liquor); commercial fruit juices	Black tea	
OTHER			
Apple cider vinegar (organic)	All oils and fats; all vinegars except organic apple cider vinegar; all sweeteners except unrefined agave, maple syrup, non-pasteurized honey, and raw cane sugar	Unrefined agave nectar, maple syrup, non-pasteurized honey, and raw cane sugar	

SIMPLE CHANGES TO MAKE NOW

1. Reduce your sugar intake. Start reading food labels and start cutting out those foods that include sugar. Of course, you may not be able to eliminate them all, but you can work to progressively reduce the sugar quantity in your daily diet. Eat whole fresh or dried fruit; avoid fruit juices, which are very high in sugar.

2. Have protein at every meal. Good protein sources can be dairy, eggs, fish, legumes (beans), meats, nuts, poultry, quinoa, seafood, seeds, or shellfish. Lunch and dinner should be at least 25 percent protein. If you have a grain with a meal (buckwheat, bread, couscous, pasta, rice, etc.) try to have at least as much protein.

3. Try to eat at least 50 percent vegetables for both lunch and dinner. The veggies can be cooked, raw, or as a juice. Vegetable juices are good; remember that fruit juices can have too little fiber and too much sugar.

4. Eat three or four fresh fruits daily, either as a dessert or snack. If eaten as a snack, accompany with a source of protein such as nuts or cheese.

5. Eat at least three meals a day. Or snack between meals on healthy snacks like a dried fruit and nut mix, hardboiled eggs, hummus dip with vegetables, a half can of tuna, or a protein bar with at least as much protein as sugar grams.

CHAPTER NINE

Xeno what?

THIS BOOK DEALS WITH STRESS and its effects on health. However, I would be remiss if I did not address the problem of chemical overload and its effect on our health. Remember, stress is not only psychological. It can also be physical, environmental, and yes, chemical. For decades, environmentalists have been warning us about the negative impact various chemical pollutants can have on our health. Because of this, those in the natural health community continually promote the importance of consuming organically grown foods and using products made from natural ingredients. In fact, if you visit any health food store, you will see an array of chemical-free foods, beauty care, and cleaning products. Yet, even if we are vigilant in our attempt to avoid these environmental toxins, our chemical body burden continues to accumulate—often with disastrous health consequences.

I have been aware of the impact these chemicals have on the health of our planet as well as on human health for many years. The recent publication of two papers, however, underscores the severity of the problem. The first is an article in the prestigious British medical journal, *The Lancet Oncology*, on the carcinogenic potential of the multiple chemicals found in air pollution around the world. The other was an October 2013 press release from the World Health Organization's International Agency for Research on Cancer, which stated, "The air we breathe has become polluted with a mixture of cancer-causing substances." Yet, even though the message has been delivered clearly, it continues to fall on deaf ears.

XENOBIOTIC: A NOT SO NEW, NEW WORD

Not long ago scientists coined the term xenobiotics to describe the chemicals we are routinely exposed to. The term comes from the words "xenos," meaning foreign and "bios," meaning life. Basically, a xenobiotic is any chemical that is foreign to our normal biochemical makeup, and for which we do not have specific metabolic processes. In other words, the body does not have the specific tools it needs to deal with the chemical. Although some xenobiotics can be produced within our bodies, most of our exposure comes from the world around us. Some researchers suggest that we are presently burdened by as many as 100,000 manmade xenobiotics.

A number of clinical studies have found that xenobiotic chemicals affect different parts of the body in a variety of ways. For example, xenobiotics may be an important factor in the development of fibromyalgia and chronic fatigue. There is also evidence that they are directly associated with chemical sensitivities and environmental allergies. Some studies suggest that a deficiency in the body's detoxification pathways may play a role in Parkinson's disease, as well as Alzheimer's. Other studies have associated the development of respiratory tract and food allergies with improper detoxification.

Because many xenobiotics have demonstrated estrogen-like activity, they likely play a role in estrogen-dependent diseases as well. Given the increasing number of individuals suffering from the diseases mentioned previously, the role of xenobiotics—and our capacity to minimize their absorption or eliminate those that have been absorbed—has extraordinary ramifications.

SOURCES OF XENOBIOTICS

Toxicologists typically verify the dose-symptom relationship of chemicals individually. Based on these tests, they established the "acceptable" amount of various chemicals in food we eat, the air we breathe, and the water we drink. Humans, however, are exposed to a variety of chemicals in the same meal, while using the same product, or on the same day. Yet the global and cumulative effect is never evaluated.

In North America, the xenobiotic load is considerable: food additives (such as synthetic colors and flavors, as well as preservatives), fungicides, pesticides, herbicides, antibiotic or hormone residue, industrial chemicals, and even pharmaceuticals that make their way into our environment. No wonder our bodies are unable to cope!

To give you an idea of the extent of the phenomenon, let me tell you about a study in which pregnant women throughout the United States were tested for the presence of 163 different chemicals in their bodies. Researchers from the University of California, San Francisco, analyzed the data from 268 pregnant women taking part in the National Health and Nutritional Examination Survey (NHANES) 2003–2004. Surprisingly, the researchers found that 99 percent of the women had detectable levels of toxic chemicals, including some that have been banned since the 1970s. Ninety-nine percent of these women had detectable levels of perchlorate, a chemical in rocket fuel. These women also had toxic levels of the fire-retardant polybrominated diphenyl ethers (PBDEs), as well as DDT, a pesticide banned in the United States since 1972.

THE SOLUTION

Fortunately, there is a way to reduce the impact these chemicals can have on our health. The concept of detoxification has always been a part of the natural health recovery approach used by traditional health professionals. Hippocrates, the father of medicine, is known to have said, "First, do no harm." However, the second part of the Hippocratic dictum states, "Secondly, cleanse." It suggests that for Hippocrates, detoxifying was second only to not harming.

Detoxifying, or helping the body rid itself of xenobiotics, is of primary importance in reducing the "toxic" load on the body, especially when there are so many chemicals we cannot control. To do this effectively, however, it's important to follow these simple principles.

1. DETOXIFY LIGHTLY.

Because of the significant overload of xenobiotics in our modern society, it's important to undertake a light detoxification program. You don't want to stir up too many toxins at one time. Your organs of elimination—the kidneys, liver, and intestines— may not be able to handle that level of elimination all at once.

2. DETOXIFY REGULARLY.

Traditionally, herbalists have recommended detoxification twice yearly, in the spring and fall. Unfortunately, the xenobiotic overload is significantly higher today than it was when these recommendations were first adopted. Detoxifying lightly but regularly—as often as one week every month or two—may be an approach that respects the modern reality far more effectively.

3. Detoxify intelligently.

Formulas that help detoxify should not only encourage the elimination of toxins, they must also support the organs involved in the detoxification process. These formulas should have time-proven ingredients.

Milk thistle is one of the most important herbs to support detoxification. Studies show that milk thistle not only protects liver cells (hepatocytes) from chemical damage, it also encourages the healthy regeneration of liver cells.

Other traditional detoxification herbs such as dandelion root and artichoke have also shown positive effects on liver and kidney function. Finally, turmeric has demonstrated both anti-inflammatory and liver protective effects.

Certain nutrients also exhibit liver-protective or liver-supporting benefits. These include vitamin B5 (pantothenic acid), as well as magnesium, selenium, and zinc. As a precursor to the enzyme glutathione, the amino acid cysteine is essential to proper detoxification. Much of Aged Garlic Extract's effectiveness in liver support and detoxification is attributed to the presence of cysteine.

4. Eliminate exposure whenever possible.

Good health can only be achieved through a healthy lifestyle. As you've seen, regular detoxification is essential. However, learning about where xenobiotics occur and how to avoid them can also help reduce your body burden. Following are some useful suggestions.

- Avoid all artificial colors, flavors, preservatives, and sweeteners.
- Eat low on the food chain; the closer a food is to its natural state, the fewer toxins it contains.
- Eat organically grown food whenever possible.
- Select cosmetic and body care products that use natural ingredients. Avoid those that contain petroleum-based ingredients or formaldehyde-releasing chemicals.
- Avoid using chemically based household cleaners, laundry products, and air fresheners. Buy toxin-free, biodegradable products made with natural ingredients.
- Drink spring or filtered water.
- Fill your home and work environments with houseplants that absorb toxic gases from the air. Spider plants, Boston ferns, English ivy, and dracaena are easy to grow and provide natural air pollution control.

Since xenobiotics are omnipresent in our modern world, it is critical that we protect ourselves from their damaging effects. Avoiding exposure can lessen the toxins we accumulate, while routine detoxification can help us rid those stored in our bodies.

CHAPTER TEN

Your Supplement Plan
for Success

IN THIS CHAPTER, I CONCENTRATE on those vitamins, minerals, amino acids, and nutraceuticals most depleted and with greatest effect regarding physiological stress issues. While each substance could merit a chapter's worth of content, I focus on each supplement's role in helping the body deal with stress or recuperate from its negative effects.

VITAMIN B3 (NIACIN, NIACINAMIDE)

Vitamin B3 is a unique water-soluble vitamin that has a hormone quality. The body can manufacture some vitamin B3, although not adequate for all needs, from the amino acid tryptophan.

Vitamin B3 is involved in the synthesis, as well as the breakdown by the liver, of various steroidal hormones, including cortisol, testosterone, estradiol, and progesterone.

In *Orthomolecular Medicine for Physicians*, award-winning psychiatrist and one of the fathers of orthomolecular medicine and psychiatry, Dr. Abram Hoffer, suggests that vitamin B3 (niacin) should be considered as an "anti-stress" vitamin. Niacinamide, a form of vitamin B3, has also been reported to have antianxiety effects similar to benzodiazepines, a popular antianxiety drug. This, of course, may also explain part of its "anti-stress" effects.

The body needs vitamin B3 in order to metabolize proteins, fats, and carbohydrates. B3 works with the trace element chromium as part of the glucose tolerance factor (GTF) in aiding the body to use insulin effectively. This is of particular importance for a few reasons. First, insulin resistance, a side effect of the long-term stress response, is one of the causes of the metabolic syndrome, or Syndrome X. The GTF helps reduce the risk of insulin resistance. Second, improved insulin use helps control the sugar cravings often associated with insulin resistance.

Niacin is available in at least two forms: niacin and niacinamide. Niacinamide is my preferred form of vitamin B3 because it does not cause the release of histamine, often called niacin flush, caused by vitamin B3 in the form of niacin. Though niacin flush is not dangerous, it is uncomfortable and sometimes unsettling.

VITAMIN B5 (PANTOTHENIC ACID)

Vitamin B5 is converted in the body to coenzyme A (CoA). This coenzyme has a variety of roles to play in the body, from energy production to detoxification of alcohol by the liver.

This vitamin has important roles to play in regards to stress. First, pantothenic acid, another name for this vitamin, is required for the synthesis of steroid hormones, including cortisol. The importance of pantothenic acid to adrenal function is highlighted by the fact that pantothenic acid supplementation can have a curative effect of adrenal necrosis. The fact that the necrosis, or death, of adrenal cells can be prevented and even reversed using this vitamin highlights its importance for these glands. Another important effect of vitamin B5 is that is actually helps to reduce the negative effects of stress on the body.

Interestingly, the most common vitamin B5 deficiency symptoms—irritability, fatigue, and apathy—are all symptoms associated with high stress levels and "burnout."

VITAMIN C (ASCORBIC ACID)

Vitamin C is probably the best known of vitamins, thanks in great part to the work of the late Dr. Linus Pauling. Though this nutrient is actually a hormone in most animals, certain species—including non-human primates, guinea pigs, fruit bats and, yes, humans—are unable to synthesize it and therefore must get it in their diet. Its effects are wide-ranging, from being required to produce collagen and elastin, to its role in immunity, wound healing, and as an antioxidant.

What interests us here is its role in adrenal function and stress. It is interesting to note that although vitamin C is present in every part of the body, it is most concentrated in the adrenal glands. Vitamin C is required for the proper metabolism of the amino acid tyrosine, for the synthesis of the thyroid hormone thyroxin, and for the production of serotonin, adrenalin, and cortisol.

An important note to smokers: The turnover of vitamin C was shown to be 50 percent greater in smokers than in non-smokers, suggesting that smokers could require as much as twice the amount of vitamin C as do non-smokers in order to maintain the minimum amount of vitamin C required for good health. In many cases, supplementing with extra vitamin C is the only way to compensate for the important loss due to smoking.

MAGNESIUM

It is difficult to overstate magnesium's importance in human health. The significant spectrum of activity of this mineral stems from the fact that it is involved in more than 300 different enzyme systems in the body. It is required for normal muscular activity, nerve transmission, RNA and DNA synthesis, sleep initiation and maintenance, body temperature regulation, and bone and tooth health. "Magnesium is a nutritional superstar when it comes to cardiovascular disease," according to the *Drug-Induced Nutrient Depletion Handbook*.

Interestingly, a study published in a national psychiatric journal highlighted the role of magnesium deficiency in increasing the risk of anxiety and depression. Initial research is even suggesting magnesium can decrease the frequency and severity of hot flashes in menopausal women.

Unfortunately, this extremely important mineral is one of the most depleted in our diet and commonly one of the most forgotten from a clinical point of view. Our interest in magnesium stems from the fact that magnesium deficiency can lead to greater stressability. Stress can then cause increased magnesium loss. Magnesium deficiency, it should also be noted, has long been known to lead to adrenal insufficiency in susceptible individuals.

Not surprisingly, then, the list of major stress-related symptoms is interchangeable with magnesium-related deficiency symptoms:

ANXIETY/PANIC ATTACKS. Research has shown magnesium deficiency can cause anxiety. Many clinicians have reportedly used magnesium supplementation to reduce anxiety. Some researchers also suggest an association between magnesium deficiency and panic attacks as well.

ASTHMA ATTACKS. Though atopism (an inherited susceptibility to certain diseases), delayed food sensitivities and allergies play a major role in asthma, and magnesium deficiency can set the stage for accrued bronchial constriction. This can trigger an asthma attack.

BRUXISM (grinding of teeth). Bruxism, the grinding of teeth during sleep or while in stressful situations, has been associated with magnesium deficiency for decades.

DEPRESSION. Of course, depression is generally multifactorial. However, few nutrients, with the possible exception of the B vitamins, show as many positive effects on depression as magnesium.

FATIGUE. Magnesium is essential for the production of ATP, the energy triggering substance. Though one of the signs of magnesium deficiency can be hyperactivity, magnesium deficiency generally leads to fatigue.

HEADACHES. Magnesium deficiency sets the stage for headaches, and supplementation has been very effective in controlling them—especially if they are due to excess estrogen, cervical muscle tension, or high blood pressure.

HIGH BLOOD PRESSURE. Magnesium helps relax muscles, including those that control blood vessels. A magnesium deficiency can therefore cause stiffness in the blood vessels, which in turn raises blood pressure.

HIGH CHOLESTEROL. A magnesium deficiency may predispose a person to high cholesterol due to the fact that liver enzymes involved in the metabolism of cholesterol require magnesium. Furthermore, an excellent review of the scientific literature by two American researchers has suggested that magnesium is almost as effective as statin drugs to treat high cholesterol and that is has none of statin's side effects.

INSOMNIA. Magnesium is required to trigger and maintain sleep. Therefore, a magnesium deficiency can affect the duration and/or quality of sleep.

IRRITABILITY/RESTLESSNESS. Magnesium helps to relax muscles and nerves. As such, it is very effective in reducing irritability.

MIGRAINES. Magnesium deficiency sets the stage for factors that promote headaches, including neurotransmitter release and vasoconstriction. People who experience migraine headaches generally have lower levels of serum and tissue magnesium than those who do not.

MUSCLE CRAMPS. Magnesium is required for muscle and nerve relaxation. As such, magnesium deficiency often manifests itself as leg cramps, especially at night or during sleep and, in many cases, after exercise.

OSTEOPOROSIS. Magnesium is required in the metabolism of calcium and vitamin D. It is also required for the formation of hydroxyapatite, the bone mineral. As such, it plays a crucial role in bone health.

PAIN. Researchers have shown that magnesium deficiency can lead to a lowered pain threshold and that magnesium supplementation improves the sensation of pain.

When it comes to stress and magnesium, we are confronted with a vicious spiraling cycle. That is why the only way to intervene in a situation like this is with magnesium supplementation. Magnesium supplementation's positive impact on persons who have suffered or currently suffer from stress is significant. Such supplementation is one of three supplemental pillars to help individuals suffering from symptoms associated with stress.

TYROSINE

Tyrosine is a non-essential amino acid because the body can produce it from another amino acid, phenylalanine. The need for tyrosine, however, is significantly increased during stress. This amino acid is required for the synthesis of thyroxin and adrenalin, as well as the skin-pigmenting protein melanin. Low levels have been associated with depression, low blood pressure, low body temperature, and an underactive thyroid.

Tyrosine supplementation has shown excellent results, especially in reducing the physical effects of stress. In his excellent book *The Healing Nutrients Within*, Dr. Eric Braverman notes that tyrosine "deserves to be called the stress amino acid."

Individuals who suffer from recurrent migraines should not use tyrosine. Those with skin cancer or regular hypothyroidism (Grave's disease) should also avoid tyrosine. Individuals taking MAO-inhibiting antidepressants should not supplement with tyrosine.

AGED GARLIC EXTRACT

If the word panacea could be attributed to one supplement, it would be to Aged Garlic Extract (A.G.E.). Few, if any, have benefited from as many scientific studies published in major prestigious journals. None have demonstrated such a wide array of effects, all of which are supported by serious scientific studies. Over 700 scientific publications have highlighted Aged Garlic Extract's effectiveness.

Aged Garlic Extract is, along with magnesium, the most prescribed supplement at our clinic. I have been using Aged Garlic Extract for my children, patients, and myself for more than 25 years. Though I have worked with many different brands of supplements over the years, A.G.E. is the only one on which I have never wavered or changed my mind.

Aged Garlic Extract is not your regular food or food supplement garlic. This unique garlic supplement has undergone significant chemical changes through a natural aging process that takes almost two years. Kyolic A.G.E. is produced in the United States from organically grown garlic and aged in stainless steel tanks for up 20 months. During aging the natural enzymatic reactions transform the garlic into A.G.E.

This process is a bit like the transformation of grapes to wine or milk to yogurt, though the simile is far from perfect. During this aging process the harsh and irritating garlic compounds, including allicin, are converted into safe and beneficial ones. From a social point of view, A.G.E. does not have the pungent garlic "after odor," which is why it is often referred to as "sociable garlic." Mind you, I have absolutely nothing against garlic as a food. I am half Italian after all! Nevertheless, the aging process does create an entirely novel type of supplement. The image below details some of the effects of the aging process.

How Kyolic is Aged

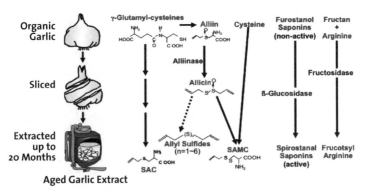

Courtesy Dr Amamgase and Wakunaga

As mentioned earlier, A.G.E. has demonstrated a wide range of effects. Though I will not bore you with the 700 or so publications that highlight Aged Garlic Extract's effectiveness, I would like to briefly mention some of its documented effects.

ANTICANCER

I am referring here to the cancer-preventative and protective effects of A.G.E., not to its therapeutic effects. Physicians have used A.G.E. as an adjunct to cancer therapy. A group of patients with inoperable cancers were given A.G.E. for six months, and their immune function was significantly improved.

ANTIOXIDANT

Aged Garlic Extract has exhibited important antioxidant activity. One of the effects is due to the presence of S-allyl cysteine, an important precursor of glutathione. The S-allyl cysteine in A.G.E. has a 98 percent absorption rate.

LIVER PROTECTANT

Aged Garlic Extract was found to protect liver cells from the toxicity of several drugs, including acetaminophen and methotrexate.

IMMUNE ENHANCEMENT

Several studies have shown A.G.E. has significant immune-enhancing activity. These effects have been demonstrated against bacteria and viruses, as well as candida albicans. Recent research undertaken at the University of Florida at Gainesville has also highlighted the immune-enhancing effectiveness of A.G.E. in reducing the severity and duration of the cold and flu.

CARDIOVASCULAR HEALTH

You will remember that one of the most detrimental effects of stress is that it increases the risk of metabolic syndrome. The symptoms of this syndrome are high blood pressure, high LDL cholesterol, low HDL, high triglycerides, and elevated blood sugar. A.G.E. is an invaluable tool when it comes to addressing metabolic syndrome. Research on A.G.E. has demonstrated its ability to normalize blood pressure in patients with uncontrolled hypertension.

Research undertaken by Matthew Budoff, MD, has demonstrated that A.G.E. helps reduce calcium buildup in the coronary artery, lowers inflammation of the arteries, improves blood vessel function, and decreases the amount of metabolically active fat tissue surrounding the heart. Many studies have also shown that A.G.E. lowers LDL cholesterol and increases the good cholesterol in ways that are similar to those of statin drugs. Furthermore, in animal model studies, Aged Garlic Extract was able to lower stress-induced blood sugar as well as reduce the complications of diabetes itself. A.G.E. was also shown to reduce fatigue and increase vitality, and interesting effect for those who are or have been affected by stress. In a clinical study in Japan, hospitalized patients showed improved stress symptoms related to their conditions after intake of A.G.E., as well as vitamins B1 and B12.

PROBIOTICS

One of the important negative effects of cortisol is its effect on the gastrointestinal bacteria, you've certainly heard them mentioned as probiotics, but they are also also called microbiota. In order to understand the implications of this, I'd like to give you an idea of the importance of these "good" bacteria. The human gastrointestinal tract is covered with about 100 trillion microorganisms, most of which are bacteria, all of which play an important role in maintaining health. Our relationship with these microorganisms is synergistic. We provide them with food and an environment in which to live and they in turn support us in a variety of ways.

Intestinal microorganisms have a wide range of useful functions. Unfortunately, the scope of this book doesn't permit me to do justice to all of their positive effects. However, a brief review will help you understand their very important preventative and curative roles. The microbiota help break down and digest lactose. And probiotic supplements have been used to help lactase-deficient individuals digest lactose. These microorganisms are essential for proper immune function. Research has shown that they can reduce the severity and duration of the cold and flu and reduce the recurrence of urinary tract infections. Several researchers have actually suggested that the excess use of antibiotics at an early age increases the risk of allergies because of its harmful effects on the microbiota. This may explain that the increase in allergies seems to follow the increased use of antibiotics in virtually all industrialized countries. Of course many of these "good" bacteria can slow the growth or even kill off harmful, pathogenic bacteria and yeast. The microbiota produces certain vitamins such as biotin and vitamin K. Furthermore the role of these good bacteria on mood and behavior cannot be overestimated. Indeed, the microbiota is involved in brain development, as well as in the production of neurotransmitters such as serotonin. The quality and composition of the microbiota may even influence body composition. Probiotic supplements have also shown very positive effects on improving premenstrual tension symptoms as well. The presence of these "good" bacteria has also been shown to reduce the risk of cardiovascular disease. Finally, the positive effects of probiotics on irritable bowel syndrome, a condition commonly found in persons who are undergoing or have undergone important stress, is well documented.

It is easy to understand from this limited review that the effects of our gut bacteria, or microbiota, are wide ranging. Though some research has shown that stress can alter the microflora thereby reducing its effectiveness, a significant amount of research has demonstrated that these bacteria can actually reduce many of the negative effects of stress, including anxiety. Furthermore, our modern environment is filled with substances that can alter our normal gut bacteria. These include prescription antibiotics as well as antibiotic residues in our food, excess alcohol and sugar, and many chemical additives. The use of probiotic supplements can therefore be very helpful as part of a supplement program to help individuals maintain or recover optimal health. This is especially true for those who are recovering from Syndrome S.

The two probiotic supplements that I have recommended the most in helping patients improve their "good" bacteria are Bio-K +, a well researched, fermented milk product with very high levels of beneficial bacteria, and Kyo-Dophilus. The latter is manufactured by Wakunaga of America, the makers of Aged Garlic Extract. Kyo-Dophilus is a unique probiotic supplement in many ways. My interest in it was sparked by a conversation I had over 20 years ago with my friend, the late Charlie Fox. Charlie was so impressed by Kyo-Dophilus that his excitement became almost contagious, as it always was. I decided to research this product and try it myself. Here are a few points I'd like to make about Kyo-Dophilus and why it is so effective.

Kyo-Dophilus contains bacteria strains of human origin. This is important since these strains have a higher affinity for colonizing the human intestinal tract than non-human strains. Furthermore, their strains have been shown to withstand and survive the acidity of the stomach. Indeed, there is little point in an individual taking a probiotic supplement if the bacteria in it are not alive upon consumption, or if the organisms simply die when they encounter the harshly acidic environment of the stomach. Bacteria need to reach the small and large intestines intact to 'set up shop' and proliferate before they are able to confer their benefits. Rather than using a smorgasbord of bacteria, some of which have little or no value to humans, Kyo-Dophilus supplies a few specially-selected, scientifically researched, acid-resistant strains of probiotic bacteria. These strains have been shown to colonize the human GI tract effectively and have demonstrated a variety of clinical benefits in humans. Finally, the bacteria in Kyo-Dophilus have undergone a special proprietary process and extensive testing to ensure that they are stable at room temperature. This is very important from a compliance point of view. People generally have all their pill bottles, prescription or over the counter, lined up together somewhere. It's hard to forget one when they are all there together. I have found, however, that since almost all probiotic supplements need refrigeration, patients often forget to take them because they don't notice them. The fact that Kyo-Dophilus does not need refrigeration and can be placed with the other supplements or with the prescription medication ensures a far greater compliance. One less stress!

NUTRIENTS AND HERBS

A variety of other natural supplements have been shown to be useful in supporting the body during stress. For these substances, appropriate use depends on individual needs, and I encourage you to work with your healthcare provider to determine the right plan.

5-HTP	5-HTP, or 5-hydroxy tryptophan, is the immediate precursor of serotonin. As such, it may help alleviate serotonin deficits such as depression, insomnia, and increased perception of pain.
Adrenal extracts	Adrenal extracts are dried extracts of adrenal cortex tissue. These extracts have been used for decades as an "organ specific" treatment of adrenal fatigue.
Ashwagandha	Ashwagandha, sometimes called Indian ginseng, is traditionally considered an adaptogenic herb. Adaptogens are substances that help the body in adapting to biological, emotional, environmental, or physical stressors. This herb has also been used for inducing sleep.
Chromium	Chromium is a cofactor with vitamin B3 as part of the glucose tolerance factor (GTF). As such, it helps sensitize the body's cells to insulin. It also helps in preventing or reversing metabolic syndrome and helps reduce cravings for sugars or other carbohydrates.
Eleuthero-coccus	Also referred to as Siberian ginseng, Eleutherococcus is one of the most versatile and safest adaptogenic herbs. It improves resistance to stress and increases energy and immunity.

GABA	Gamma amino butyric acid, or GABA, is actually the natural counterpart of the drug gabapentin. It is effective as an antidepressant and as a sleep aid as well. It should be noted that natural GABA does not have the side effects of its synthetic counterpart.
Relora	Relora is a proprietary blend of two herbs: *Phellodendron amurense (P. amurense)*, and magnolia. Its main effect regarding stress is in reducing excess cortisol. In doing so, Relora helps normalize DHEA levels and reduce sugar and salt cravings when under stress.
Theanine	Theanine is an amino acid found in green tea. This amino acid helps increase alpha brain waves, the electrical brain waves associated with relaxation.
Rhodiola	Rhodiola is an adaptogenic herb that has been used for centuries to combat fatigue by increasing physical endurance and exercise performance. As an adaptogen, it also speeds recovery from illness.

SIMPLE CHANGES TO MAKE NOW

At our clinic, we use a vitamin supplement with high levels of vitamin B3 and B5, vitamin C, and magnesium to support individuals dealing with important periods of stress. A.G.E. is also an important supplement to help offset the effects of stress.

1. Take 100–200 mg of magnesium, as magnesium citrate, glycinate, or chelate, daily. For sleep issues, take magnesium in the evening or at bedtime.

2. Take a B complex supplying 25–75 mg of the B vitamins. Whenever possible, you can take higher levels of vitamins

B5 and B3. Ideally, the vitamin B3 should be in the form of niacinamide. Do not exceed 75 mg of either vitamin B5 or B3 unless recommended by a health professional.

3. Take 600–1,000 mg of Aged Garlic Extract (A.G.E.) daily as an immune-enhancing, cardioprotective supplement.

4. It is best to consult with a health professional trained in nutritional medicine to develop a personalized nutrition program.

"I DON'T NEED TO TAKE SUPPLEMENTS; I EAT WELL."

When I suggest the use of food supplements as an addition to a healthy diet, most patients will initially say, "I don't need to take supplements; I eat well." I'd like to address this myth.

Taking supplements should never replace eating real, high-quality, unprocessed foods. However, adding food supplements to the diet is increasingly necessary when it comes to achieving, maintaining, or recovering optimal health. Indeed, an increasing number of factors justify the intelligent use of food supplements.

1. FOODS ARE NOT AS NUTRITIOUS AS THEY ONCE WERE. Some reports suggest that in some cases, from 30 to 100 percent of certain nutrients may have been lost in our foods.*

   - Conventional commercial agriculture has depleted the soils.
   - We are consuming an increasingly significant amount of frozen or prepared foods.
   - Fruits and vegetables are not always picked when ripe.

- Foods are warehoused for longer periods of time.
- Refining foods causes significant nutrient depletion.
- Animals are raised industrially (factory farming).
- Much of this points to the value of purchasing locally grown food products from small family farms as well as organically grown produce from reliable suppliers.

2. OUR NEED FOR PROTECTIVE NUTRIENTS HAS INCREASED BECAUSE OF:

- Increased environmental pollution
- Chemical additives
- Accrued stress, without the ability to fight or flee
- Smoking
- Alcohol consumption
- Increased use of drugs and enhancing substances in animal feed (antibiotics, hormones)

3. THE INCREASED USE OF DRUGS ALSO INCREASES THE NEED FOR VARIOUS NUTRIENTS.

This point, among others, is highlighted in the Drug-Induced Nutrient Depletion Handbook, in which the author notes, "It was amazing to uncover the large number of studies appearing in the scientific literature reporting the drug-induced depletion of nutrients."

All of this justifies the comment by Dr. David Heber, Professor, UCLA Department of Medicine:

"We now have a substantial body of data showing that if everyone took a few supplements every day, they could significantly lower their risk of a multitude of serious diseases."

CHAPTER ELEVEN

Exercise Plan for Stress Management

ACCORDING TO THE MOST RECENT Stress in America survey conducted by the American Psychological Association (APA), 20 percent of Americans self-report "extreme" or "high" stress levels. More than 60 percent of this group says they do not manage stress well and turn instead to coping methods such as napping, eating, or drinking alcohol. Not surprisingly, given the cumulative effects of poorly managed stress, respondents in this group are far more likely to report increasing levels of stress year after year.

In previous chapters, we've discussed the differences between "good" and "bad" stress. Chronic and/or unmitigated stress can cause a wide variety of negative physiological and psychological effects. These include challenges to the cardiovascular, digestive, neurological, and lymphatic systems. Physical symptoms can include headaches, upset stomach, high blood pressure, chest pain, general body pain, or trouble sleeping.

"Good" stress, on the other hand, can keep us energized, focused, and motivated. One recent animal study links short-term stress to new nerve cell proliferation and increased memory. Many clinical trials currently underway explore positive effects of stress on the body and mind. We're likely to see more proof of similar connections in the next few decades.

Physical exercise can put stress on the body. In most cases, however, it provides the kind of good stress our bodies welcome. Ironically, however, some of my patients experience stress when I even broach the topic of exercise. For those accustomed to sedentary life, any encouragement to "get moving" can feel confrontational.

I offer two pieces of good news:

1. When it comes to stress, the benefits of physical activity are indisputable and very reliable.

2. The level of exercise necessary to realize these benefits may be easier and more accessible than you imagine.

HOW DOES EXERCISE HELP WITH STRESS?

Exercise can have an immediate positive effect on stress levels. We've all experienced the benefits of fresh air, movement, increased blood flow, and "vacation" from worry after a nice hike in the beautiful outdoors. In fact, just taking time for ourselves can adjust our perception of our problems and worries.

In the longer term, exercise helps mitigate the negative effects of chronic stress. Exercise can help repair some of the physiological damage caused by stress. These repairs help the body manage and respond to current and future stress more effectively.

THE CARDIOVASCULAR SYSTEM

Exercise helps correct some of the damage chronic stress can cause to the heart and arteries by enhancing exercise tolerance, reducing body weight, lowering blood pressure and "bad" LDL cholesterol, and increasing "good" HDL cholesterol.

THE ENDOCRINE SYSTEM

Chronic stress can lead to insulin resistance, which is associated with metabolic syndrome and type II diabetes. Exercise increases insulin sensitivity, which reduces the amount of insulin that is secreted by the pancreas and improves the efficiency of glucose metabolism.

THE LYMPHATIC SYSTEM

Exercise improves the health of the lymphatic system, which can be compromised by toxicities and muscle tension produced from chronic stress.

THE MUSCULOSKELETAL SYSTEM

Exercise helps maintain and/or increase bone mass while increasing muscle strength and tone.

THE BRAIN

Exercise can help reverse neurochemical imbalances caused by chronic stress. As discussed in previous chapters, chronic stress can cause the malfunction and depletion of neurotransmitters such as norepinephrine, dopamine, and serotonin. Exercise increases norepinephrine levels and protects against its depletion. Norepinephrine itself is important to proper brain function. It is known to modulate or play a role in the action of serotonin and dopamine. Both serotonin and dopamine are associated with elevated mood, memory, and learning.

These are only a few examples of the benefits of exercise. There is really no physiological system that does not benefit from exercise. That fact may be the key to the combined impacts of exercise for people suffering from chronic stress. The

American Psychological Association describes this synergy in the following way:

> [Exercise] forces the body's physiological systems—all of which are involved in the stress response—to communicate much more closely than usual. The cardiovascular system communicates with the renal system, which communicates with the muscular system. And all of these are controlled by the central and sympathetic nervous systems, which also must communicate with each other. This workout of the body's communication system may be the true value of exercise. In other words, the more sedentary we get, the less efficient our bodies are in responding to stress.

I'M SOLD! BUT WHAT EXERCISE SHOULD I DO?

Do what you love! This can mean any kind of movement that gets your heart pumping faster: walking, climbing stairs, yoga, tai chi, gardening, swimming, or even cleaning the house. It's better to exercise more frequently and at a lower intensity, so try to find an activity you can build into your daily schedule.

Find an exercise buddy to increase the odds you'll stick with your new activity. If you know your buddy is waiting for you at the gym or trailhead, you're that much less likely to bail on your plan. Sharing your goals with another person (and asking for their support) also increases your accountability.

Remember, it's never too late to start, and you have many choices. The important thing is to move daily for at least 30 minutes. Studies show a reduction in mortality rates even for those who begin exercising after 40. Of course, if you have not been physically active in some time or suffer from any chronic condition, consult with your physician before beginning a new exercise program.

A NOTE ON WALKING

Walking is probably the easiest, safest, and least expensive way to exercise. If you choose walking as your exercise activity, make sure to walk at least 10,000 steps per day. This is considered "physically active." Taking 12,500 steps per day is considered "highly active!"

How to count your steps? A pedometer ($12 and up) is a small device that counts your steps for you. Attach it to your belt or waistband before starting your day, and it will keep a tally of the steps you take. There are also pedometer-type apps available for your iOS or Android smart phones.

A NOTE ON WEIGHT LIFTING

Weight lifting benefits can come from the resistance you get from your own body weight, free weights (typically dumbbells), or weight machines. An inexpensive way to get a weight-bearing workout is to leverage your own body weight with push-ups, chin-ups, and squats. If you have access to a gym you'll find muscle-targeted exercise machines and full-body circuits designed without any free weights. At the gym, you can also often take advantage of support and guidance from professional trainers.

To keep things easy and safe, I've included a set of just three exercises designed to work 80 percent of body muscle mass. Dr. Michael Hewitt, research director for exercise science at Canyon Ranch Health Resort, developed the sequence below to be performed in about 10 to 15 minutes. Start with five-pound dumbbells and increase only when you can complete all sets easily with proper form.

CHEST PRESSES

Lie on your back, knees bent. Hold your dumbbells with elbows bent out to the sides, shoulder height, and bring them together up above your chest. Slowly lower your elbows to the starting position, then repeat.

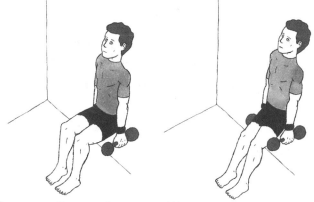

STANDING SQUATS AGAINST A WALL

With feet hip distance apart, hold your dumbbells with arms hanging straight at your sides. Slowly squat until your hips are level with your knees—but not below your knees. Your feet must be far enough out from the wall so that when you squat, your knees are not farther forward than your toes. Return to a standing position and repeat.

ONE-ARM DUMBBELL ROW

Place one knee and one hand on a chair or bench. Bend the standing leg. Hold the weight in your other arm and let it hang straight down. Then bring your elbow up close to your side and control it down. Keep your back flat. Think of sawing a big log as you bring your elbow up and down. Keep your elbow close to your body. Exhale as you lift. Inhale as you lower.

A NOTE ON RUNNING

When my patients ask me about running, I offer an answer dedicated runners sometimes don't like. Some research indicates sustained, frequent, and high-intensity endurance exercise can actually have adverse effects on our cardiovascular health and immunity. Of course, these effects can have a cascading impact on or exacerbate the effects of stress.

I counsel patients managing the effects of chronic stress, including overtaxed adrenals, to avoid high-intensity endurance training. Once health and balance is restored, appropriate running mileage can restart.

SIMPLE CHANGES YOU CAN MAKE NOW

1. Get moving! Aim for 30 minutes of activity per day. Remember, you can split this time into three periods of 10 minutes each if necessary. Making this effort will not only decrease your current level of stress, but will also help repair damage from years of chronic stress.

2. Try to walk at least 10,000 steps daily. Get a pedometer to track your progress and stay motivated.

3. Complete some form of weight-bearing exercise at least three times per week. I've included the "Key Three" exercises above, but any type of strength training using your own body weight, free weights, or weight machines will be beneficial. Optional: It's not necessary by any means, but if you can afford it, hire a personal trainer. This can provide both investment motivation and a solid foundation if you need it.

CHAPTER TWELVE

Your Meditation Plan for Stress

OUR NEW DIGITAL WORLD MEANS that we are always on. Modern technology, with its relentless and constant demands on our time and attention, is a significant contributor to stress. Among American adults, 91 percent own a cell phone. Of this group, 56 percent own "smart" phones. 29 percent report their phone as the first and last thing they look at every day—something they "couldn't live without." Forty-four percent of users sleep with their phone by their side so as not to miss a message, text, tweet, or other update.

In another study, 26 percent of respondents said they would feel guilty if they don't promptly respond to work-related messages outside of business hours. For many of us, this new 24/7 world is a significant source of ongoing stress. Remember, our bodies cannot differentiate between the apprehension we feel seeing an email from the boss and the sudden appearance of a man-eating beast. Both release a jolt of adrenaline and cortisol.

Mind you, the above statistics refer to adults, those "Digital Immigrants" who knew the world before the technological revolution. Today's children have an even more pressing problem. Those born after the year 2000 have never experienced a world without omnipresent technology. Because of this, we call their generation "Digital Natives."

A native environment filled with electronic games, computers, Wi-Fi, smart phones, and tablets causes me serious concern. In some ways these devices have made life easier. But they also present a significant challenge to balanced brain activity as they continually increase stress. Only time will tell what the effects of our current technological environment will be on growing brains and bodies.

For instance, electronic games offer an escape into a fantasy world, and some look like a great deal of fun. Unfortunately, most stimulate the stress response in an unhealthy way. The virtual danger a player feels fleeing for his or her life, killing an enemy, or racing (and crashing) a car is indistinguishable from reality. During the course of these games, the sympathetic nervous system activates and releases adrenaline. The "adrenaline rush" kids may talk about in jest is real.

The difference between virtual war games and the games we played as children is important to note. When we play outside, instead of in front of a screen, we respond to perceived play-stress in the same way. The sympathetic nervous system is activated. Outside, however, we actually do "fight or flee," and our bodies process adrenaline and blood sugar in an appropriate manner. This does not happen when the only physical movement is hands on a joystick.

What's worse, video games can be addictive for males in particular. The games activate the dopamine-related reward response area of the brain in a way that compels continued play. I believe these games will not only keep our children inactive and unhealthy, but also result in a decreased sensitivity to killing and dying. This might be related to the increased school violence we've seen over the past few decades.

This same reward response activates with the "ding" of a new text or email. Dopamine causes "seeking" behavior, increasing arousal and interest. We feel satisfied when we read and respond to the message. The loop occurring when this happens over and over keeps us online and glued to our phone. The end result is constant stimulation and attention shifts—which creates chronic stress.

Of course kids aren't only online playing games. By two years of age, nearly 50 percent of all babies have used a computer or mobile device. Most young people have a smart phone by the age of 13. You rarely see a teenager actually talking on the phone, because they are more likely to be texting, tweeting, or posting on social media. These social networks themselves can promote stress.

Recent research in the journal *Computers in Human Behavior* reports on a phenomenon that kids call FoMO, or fear of missing out. FoMO proves to be a trigger for increased and more anxious use of social networks. Study participants with high FoMO were more likely to check social media sites during class and, frighteningly, while driving. This particular study involved young people, but I know many adults who can identify and relate.

BREAK THE TECHNOLOGY HABIT

Technology stress is real. For those suffering from chronic stress, I recommend the following strategies to reduce and mitigate negative impact:

- Schedule "device-free" periods during which you don't engage with any screen or online activity. Expect that this will be difficult. To increase success, prepare alternate activities and enlist the support of family or friends.

- Make a concerted effort to keep your smart phone and tablet out of your bedroom. Stop using your phone or computer a few hours before bedtime. The light from devices can impact the quality of your sleep.

- Set some self-imposed limits on email and social media. While at work, quit your email platform and sign out of social media networks. Make it difficult to access these when you have the urge.

- Schedule time to respond to email and let your colleagues and friends know your plan. If you do this, they won't expect an immediate response and you may feel less pressured to reply.

- If you need to be on your computer, work on only one task at a time. Keeping multiple windows open encourages multitasking and attention shifting, which can cause the release of stress hormones.

- Create face-to-face opportunities for a feeling of connection. A low-tech approach can result in a richer experience and be more satisfying.

MEDITATION AND STRESS

Are you a left or right-brained person? Chances are, you know what I mean when I ask this question. Most people associate the left side of the brain with analytical thought and link creativity to the right side. Of the two, our culture often seems to add greater value to the logical, linear, left brain activity. Putting aside value measures for now, our important takeaway is this: When it comes to stress management, balance and integration of the two sides is critical.

When we engage the left-brain, which we do most of the time, we engage the sympathetic nervous system involved in the adrenaline release. With right brain activity, we engage the parasympathetic nervous system, which causes the heart and breathing rate to slow, improves digestion, and increases blood flow. In other words, the parasympathetic nervous system involves a relaxation response. "Right brain" activity helps you relax.

Artistic activities like painting or playing music can activate the parasympathetic nervous system. Because these activities still require thought and performance, however, our left-brain activity cannot fully calm. Given this, Orthodox priest Dr. Symeon Rodger suggests the most effective way to still the mind (and improve our stress reaction) is to Sit Still and Do Nothing (SSDN).

In the west, meditation practice is often associated with eastern spirituality. East Asian spiritual leaders like Thich Nhat Hanh and the Dalai Lama are familiar to many. Virtually every global spiritual tradition, however, encourages some form of meditation practice. For almost 2,000 years, Eastern Orthodox Church members have practiced the "Jesus Prayer," also known as the "Prayer of the Heart." Benedictine monks practice Christian contemplative prayer. Native Americans believe meditation helps transcend the material world and increase divine wisdom.

If you have yet to practice meditation on a regular basis, I am here to tell you it will reduce the effects of stress and benefit your health. Researchers are still trying to determine the exact mechanisms of this process, but several studies prove meditation's positive effects.

The Shamantha Project investigated the benefits of meditation on mental and physical health. Led by researchers at the University of California, Davis, Center for Mind and Brain, it is one of the most comprehensive studies on the topic to date and has been endorsed by both the Dalai Lama and the scientific community.

As part of the project, researcher Tonya Jacobs measured the emotional and biochemical states of subjects before and after a three-month meditation retreat. Post-retreat, researchers saw clear changes. The telomerase enzyme, which is involved in cell and gene-protective telomere activity, increased significantly. Individually, participants showed an inverse correlation between self-reported mindfulness levels and cortisol levels.

According to Jacobs, "The more a person reported directing their cognitive resources to immediate sensory experience and the task at hand, the lower their resting cortisol. The idea that we can train our minds in a way that fosters healthy mental habits—and that these habits may be reflected in mind-body relations—is not new. It's been around for thousands of years across various cultures and ideologies. However, this idea is just beginning to be integrated into Western medicine as objective evidence accumulates. Hopefully, studies like this one will contribute to that effort."

A controlled eight-week mindfulness-based stress reduction program (MSRP) revealed similar correlations. In this case, participants in the University of Madison study were assigned to one of two groups. One group was trained in MSRP and the other in an active health enhancement program (HEP). Both groups showed declined cortisol levels. The MSRP group, however, showed significantly lower post-stress inflammatory reactions.

This research provides definitive proof of meditation's benefits on health. Even in its absence, I think we all know how good it feels to take a deep breath, slow down, and calm our racing minds. If you suffer from the symptoms of chronic stress, taking some time every day to "do nothing" is a simple, inexpensive, and positive start.

THREE EASY STEPS FOR BEGINNING MEDITATORS

1. Schedule time for yourself. Identify a quiet place where you won't be interrupted for 10 to 15 minutes. If you have one, set a timer for the period you want to meditate.

2. Sit comfortably with your spine straight: head over shoulders, shoulders over pelvis. Remember, you don't need to sit on the floor or cushion. If it's easier, sit upright on a chair. Just be sure to follow the above instructions and keep your legs uncrossed and feet flat on the floor.

3. Watch your breath go in and out as you breathe naturally. Let your thoughts come and go without effort or attachment. Watch them as if they were clouds moving in the sky.

Putting it all Together

I HOPE THAT WHAT I'VE SHARED provides both a better understanding of, and a sense of power over, your chronic stress symptoms. Stress is real and inevitable, and has a physiological impact that many overlook. As I've shared repeatedly, stress is not all "in your head." Chronic stress can promote the development of widely varied symptoms in multiple body systems.

The most important message I wish to deliver is one of hope. No matter what symptoms you experience—hormonal imbalances, gastrointestinal upset, aches and pains, emotional disturbances—a proper treatment plan can help reverse or eliminate these over time. Even better, you can prevent most negative effects of stress with knowledge and integrated self-care.

We often have little to no control over stressful circumstances. In fact, some events we don't even recognize as stressful. We do, however, have total control over the foods we eat and avoid. Our lifestyle—including sleep quality, technology use, and meditation—are also largely under our direction. Finally, we can control how we respond to and manage the effects of stress.

I've shared patient successes along with nutrition and exercise recommendations specific to stress management. Not surprisingly, good choices for stress management are those that also reduce the risks of cancer, heart disease, and dementia.

These choices also promote increased mental and physical energy. You have nothing to lose and everything to gain. I wish you good luck and even better health!

HOW ARE THEY NOW?

A couple of months after our initial consultation, Cathy experienced many changes, all of them positive. She and her husband had gone to see a marriage counselor to help with their relationship. Now, the two of them take one weekend off every month to spend quality time together with no email or smart phone, and no teenage son.

Cathy has also made a number of dietary changes. She has significantly reduced the amount of sugar in her diet. She is also eating more protein. Most importantly, Cathy is avoiding foods that we discovered she was intolerant to. This has radically improved her irritable bowel syndrome, as well as her overall health. A personalized supplement program helped increase Cathy's energy levels while also improving her sleep. As her sleep improved, so did her memory and concentration.

Cathy also realized she was not superwoman. Today, she maintains an effective exercise program, training at the gym three times a week. She walks 10,000 steps daily on those days when she does not train. Although Cathy knows she has to exercise, she also knows that she must not overdo it. As a result, Cathy looks and feels 10 years younger than when I first met her. She knows that stress is a fact of life, but she also knows now how she can help her body to cope with the stressors she cannot avoid. The name of the game, she told me, is health empowerment.

Jerry has lost 25 pounds to date. While that is not as much as he expected, he is encouraged by the other changes. With dietary modifications, nutritional supplements including Aged Garlic Extract, and right-brain activity, he has experienced a drop in both his blood sugar and cholesterol levels. He also told me that family and friends have noticed that he does not over-react any more.

The last time we met, Jerry commented that, before dealing with his stress issue, he never felt truly rested, even after sleeping for long hours. Now, however, he feels totally refreshed when he wakes up. His mind is clear, and he now looks forward to the coming workday. Interestingly, Jerry hasn't reduced his workload. He just works smarter—and he knows how to reduce the impact of stress on his body. Same stress, less damage.

Pat finally gave birth to a 7-pound baby boy. Of course, her fertility problems did not disappear overnight. Some of the improvements associated with her lifestyle took months, or even years. Pat had her hormone levels tested. She was put on a nutritional program to improve her stress reactions and to correct an imbalance between her cortisol and progesterone levels. A physician also prescribed a low dose of progester-one in order to improve her hormone balance. After just a few months, Pat was able to discontinue the hormone replacement. In addition, the amino acid tyrosine was used as a supplement to help improve her thyroid function. Pat also started exercis-ing—rebounding on a mini trampoline for 20 minutes a day, five days a week. As her hormonal health improved, so did her PMS and her fertility. Things also got better at work. Three years after starting treatment, Pat became pregnant.

Pat is now doing very well, though she admits that having a baby does limit the amount of sleep she gets. She now walks on her mini-trampoline with her baby in her arms—the motion puts him to sleep. And, though Pat is getting less sleep these days, she has more energy in the morning than ever before.

———————

Working with Luke was not easy. This very intelligent young man questioned every recommendation I made. Because of his sensitive emotional nature and continual questioning, it took Luke a year to finally get on the program and make the changes he needed to help manage his stress. I recommended that he significantly reduce the carbohydrates in his diet while increasing his protein intake. His diet consisted of lots of vegetables, a good amount of protein, and very few carbohydrates. Luke was put on a nutritional supplement program that included tyrosine, as well as magnesium and niacinamide for their anxiolytic effects. He has also begun to exercise moderately, focusing primarily on a weight-bearing exercise program. Because of Luke's personality and physiology, he cannot do high-impact aerobic exercises. An intense aerobic workout would overstimulate an already overstimulated system.

As we speak, Luke is transformed. He very rarely has anxiety attacks. When he does, he knows why they occur and what he can do to manage them. The last time I met Luke he was excited about an upcoming movie project and television series he was taping. Excited, but not overexcited.

References

Abbasi B, Kimiagar M, Sadeghniiat K, Shirazi MM, Hedayati M, Rashidkhani B. The effect of magnesium supplementation on primary insomnia in elderly: A double-blind placebo-controlled clinical trial. *J Res Med Sci.* 2012;17(12):1161-9.

American Psychological Association. *Stress in America: Missing the Health Care Connection.* Washington, DC: American Psychological Association;2013. http://www.apa.org/news/press/releases/stress/2012/full-report.pdf. Accessed January 3, 2014.

Ahmad MS, Ahmed N. Antiglycation properties of aged garlic extract: possible role in prevention of diabetic complications. *J Nutr.* 2006;136(3 Suppl):796S-799S.

Altura BM, Altura BT. Tension headaches and muscle tension: is there a role for magnesium?. *Med Hypotheses.* 2001;57(6):705-13.

Amagase H. Clarifying the real bioactive constituents of garlic. *J Nutr.* 2006;136(3 Suppl):716S-725S.

Anderson CA, Bushman BJ. Effects of violent video games on aggressive behavior, aggressive cognition, aggressive affect, physiological arousal, and prosocial behavior: a meta-analytic review of the scientific literature. *Psychol Sci.* 2001;12(5):353-9.

Benefits of exercise—reduces stress, anxiety, and helps fight depression, from Harvard Men's Health Watch. Harvard Health Publications Web site. http://www.health.harvard.edu/press_releases/benefits-of-exercisereduces-stress-anxiety-and-helps-fight-depression. Published February 2011. Accessed December 31, 2013.

Berridge KC, Robinson TE. What is the role of dopamine in reward: hedonic impact, reward learning, or incentive salience?. *Brain Research Reviews.* 1998 Dec;28(3):309-69.

Blodget H. American per-capita sugar consumption hits 100 pounds per year. Business Insider Web site. http://www.businessinsider.com/chart-american-sugar-consumption-2012-2. Published February 19, 2012. Accessed December 31, 2013.

Borek C. Antioxidant health effects of aged garlic extract. *J Nutr.* 2001;131(3s):1010S-5S.

Borek C. Health benefits of aged garlic extract. *Townsend Letter for Doctors & Patients.* August-Sept 2004.

Boudarene M, Legros JJ, Timsit-Berthier M. Study of the stress response: role of anxiety, cortisol and DHEAs. *Encephale.* 2002 Mar-Apr;28(2):139-46.

Brandt M. Video games activate reward regions of brain in men more than women, Stanford study finds. *EurekAlert.* http://www.eurekalert.org/pub_releases/2008-02/sumc-vga020408.php. Accessed January 3, 2014.

Braverman E. *The healing nutrients within: facts, findings, and new research on amino acids*. 3rd ed. North Bergen, NJ : Basic Health Publications; 2003.

Bremner D, Vermetten E, Kelley ME. Cortisol, dehydroepiandrosterone, and estradiol measured over 24 hours in women with childhood sexual abuse-related posttraumatic stress disorder. *J Nerv Ment Dis*. 2007;195(11):919-27.

Brenner J. Pew internet: mobile. *Pew Research Center*. http://pewinternet.org/Commentary/2012/February/Pew-Internet-Mobile.aspx. Accessed January 1, 2014.

Brunkhorst WK, Hess EL. An interaction of cortisol with components of lymphatic tissue. *Biochem Biophys Res Commun*. 1961 June 28;5(3): 238-42.

Bucci LR. *Nutrition Applied to Injury Rehabilitation and Sports Medicine*. Boca Raton, FL: CRC Press; 1994.

Budoff MJ, Ahmadi N, Gul KM, et al. Aged garlic extract supplemented with B vitamins, folic acid and L-arginine retards the progression of subclinical atherosclerosis: a randomized clinical trial. *Prev Med*. 2009;49(2-3):101-7.

Cohen S, Janicki-Deverts D, Miller GE. Psychological stress and disease. *JAMA*. 2007;298(14):1685-7.

Common Sense Media. Zero to Eight: Children's Media Use in America 2013. *Common Sense Media Web Site*. http://www.commonsensemedia.org/sites/default/files/research/zero-to-eight-2013.pdf. Accessed January 3, 2013.

Davis DR. Declining fruit and vegetable nutrient composition: what is the evidence?. *HortScience*. 2009 February;44(1):15-19.

Deans E. Magnesium and the brain: the original chill pill. *Psychology Today Web Site*. http://www.psychologytoday.com/blog/evolutionary-psychiatry/201106/magnesium-and-the-brain-the-original-chill-pill. Published June 12, 2011. Accessed December 31, 2013.

De Rouffignac C, Quamme G. Renal magnesium handling and its hormonal control. *Physiol Rev*. 1994;74(2):305-22.

De Vrese M, Winkler P, Rautenberg P, et al. Effect of Lactobacillus gasseri PA 16/8, Bifidobacterium longum SP 07/3, B. bifidum MF 20/5 on common cold episodes: a double blind, randomized, controlled trial. *Clin Nutr*. 2005;24(4):481-91.

Dinan TG, Cryan JF. Regulation of the stress response by the gut microbiota: implications for psychoneuroendocrinology. *Psychoneuroendocrinology*. 2012;37(9):1369-78.

Dingle P. Stress cycle. *NOVA: Australia's Holistic Journal Web Site*. http://www.novamagazine.com.au/article_archive/2012/2012-03-the-stress-cycle.html. Accessed December 31, 2013.

Dishman RK. Brain monoamines, exercise, and behavioral stress: animal models. *Med Sci Sports Exerc*. 1997;29(1):63-74.

Drewnowski A, Almiron-Roig, E. Human perceptions and preferences for fat-rich foods. In: Montmayeur JP, le Coutre J, eds. *Fat Detection: Taste, Texture, and Post Ingestive Effects*. Boca Raton, FL: CRC Press; 2010.

Fredricks DN. *The Human Microbiota: How Microbial Communities Affect Health and Disease*. Hoboken, NJ: Wiley-Blackwell;2013.

Ganmaa D, Sato A. The possible role of female sex hormones in milk from pregnant cows in the development of breast, ovarian and corpus uteri cancers. *Med Hypotheses*. 2005;65(6):1028-37.

Garrison SR, Allan GM, Sekhon RK, Musini VM, Khan KM. Magnesium for skeletal muscle cramps. *Cochrane Database Syst Rev.* 2012;9:CD009402.

Graci S, Crisafi D. *Les Superaliments, Une Moisson D'Energie Qui Peut Changer Votre Vie.* Montréal: Chenelière/McGraw-Hill;1998.

Guyton AC, Hall JE. *Textbook of Medical Physiology.* Philadelphia, PA: Elsevier Saunders;2006.

Gwilt PR, Lear CL, Tempero MA, et al. The effect of garlic extract on human metabolism of acetaminophen. *Cancer Epidemiol Biomarkers Prev.* 1994;3(2):155-60.

Hoffer A. *Orthomolecular Medicine for Physicians.* New Canaan, CT: Keats Pub;1989.

Holub WR. Do allergic reactions represent hypersensitivity or nutritionally deficient detoxification?. *Journal of Applied Nutrition.* 1979;31(3/4): 67-74.

Imai J, Ide N, Nagae S, Moriguchi T, Matsuura H, Itakura Y. Antioxidant and radical scavenging effects of aged garlic extract and its constituents. *Planta Med.* 1994;60(5):417-20.

Ishikawa H, Saeki T, Otani T, et al. Aged garlic extract prevents a decline of NK cell number and activity in patients with advanced cancer. *J Nutr.* 2006;136(3 Suppl):816S-820S.

Isolauri E, Salminen S. Probiotics: use in allergic disorders: a Nutrition, Allergy, Mucosal Immunology, and Intestinal Microbiota (NAMI) Research Group Report. *J Clin Gastroenterol.* 2008;42 Suppl 2:S91-6.

Itoh K, Kawasaka T, Nakamura M. The effects of high oral magnesium supplementation on blood pressure, serum lipids and related variables in apparently healthy Japanese subjects. *Br J Nutr.* 1997;78(5):737-50.

Ivarsson M, Anderson M, Åkerstedt T, Lindblad F. The effect of violent and nonviolent video games on heart rate variability, sleep, and emotions in adolescents with different violent gaming habits. *Psychosom Med.* 2013;75(4):390-6.

Jacka FN, Overland S, Stewart R, Tell GS, Bjelland I, Mykletun A. Association between magnesium intake and depression and anxiety in community-dwelling adults: the Hordaland Health Study. *Aust N Z J Psychiatry.* 2009;43(1):45-52.

Jacobs TL, Epel ES, Lin J, et al. Intensive meditation training, immune cell telomerase activity, and psychological mediators. *Psychoneuroendocrinology.* 2011;36(5):664-81.

Jacobs TL, Shaver PR, Epel ES, et al. Self-reported mindfulness and cortisol during a Shamatha meditation retreat. *Health Psychol.* 2013;32(10):1104-9.

Kasuga S, Ushijima M, Morihara N, Itakura Y, Nakata Y. [Effect of aged garlic extract (AGE) on hyperglycemia induced by immobilization stress in mice]. *Nippon Yakurigaku Zasshi.* 1999;114(3):191-7.

Kennedy MJ, Volz PA. Ecology of Candida albicans gut colonization: inhibition of Candida adhesion, colonization, and dissemination from the gastrointestinal tract by bacterial antagonism. *Infect Immun.* 1985;49(3):654-63.

Kirby ED, Muroy SE, Sun WG, et al. Acute stress enhances adult rat hippocampal neurogenesis and activation of newborn neurons via secreted astrocytic FGF2. *eLife.* 2013;2:e00362.

Kojima R, Toyama Y, Ohnishi ST. Protective effects of an aged garlic extract on doxorubicin-induced cardiotoxicity in the mouse. *Nutr Cancer.* 1994;22(2):163-73.

Kotsirilos V, Vitetta L, Sali A. *A Guide to Evidence-Based Integrative and Complementary Medicine*. Sydney, Australia: Elsevier Churchill Livingstone;2011.

Kutsky RJ. *Handbook of Vitamins, Minerals and Hormones*. 2nd ed. New York: Van Nostrand Reinhold;1981.

Langewitz W, Rüddel H, Schächinger H. Reduced parasympathetic cardiac control in patients with hypertension at rest and under mental stress. *Am Heart J.* 1994;127(1):122-8.

Larijani VN, Ahmadi N, Zeb I, Khan F, Flores F, Budoff M. Beneficial effects of aged garlic extract and coenzyme Q10 on vascular elasticity and endothelial function: the FAITH randomized clinical trial. *Nutrition*. 2013;29(1):71-5.

Liska DJ. The detoxification enzyme systems. *Altern Med Rev*. 1998;3(3):187-98.

Liu L, Yeh YY. S-alk(en)yl cysteines of garlic inhibit cholesterol synthesis by deactivating HMG-CoA reductase in cultured rat hepatocytes. *J Nutr.* 2002;132(6):1129-34.

Loomis D, Grosse Y, Lauby-Secretan B, et al. The carcinogenicity of outdoor air pollution. *The Lancet Oncology*. 2013;14(13):1262-1263.

Maldonado PD, Alvarez-idaboy JR, Aguilar-gonzález A, et al. Role of allyl group in the hydroxyl and peroxyl radical scavenging activity of S-allylcysteine. *J Phys Chem B*. 2011;115(45):13408-17.

Mauskop A, Altura BM. Role of magnesium in the pathogenesis and treatment of migraines. *Clin Neurosci*. 1998;5(1):24-7.

Mayo Foundation. Fibromyalgia. *Mayo Clinic Web Site*. http://www.mayoclinic.com/health/fibromyalgia/DS00079. Accessed January 3, 2014.

McEwen BS. Protection and damage from acute and chronic stress: allostasis and allostatic overload and relevance to the pathophysiology of psychiatric disorders. *Ann N Y Acad Sci*. 2004;1032:1-7.

Moorkens G, Manuel y keenoy B, Vertommen J, Meludu S, Noe M, De leeuw I. Magnesium deficit in a sample of the Belgian population presenting with chronic fatigue. *Magnes Res*. 1997;10(4):329-37.

Muller MD, Sauder CL, Ray CA. Mental stress elicits sustained and reproducible increases in skin sympathetic nerve activity. *Physiol Rep*. 2013;1(1).

Myers J. Exercise and cardiovascular health. *Circulation*. 107(1):2e-5.

Nantz MP, Rowe CA, Muller CE, Creasy RA, Stanilka JM, Percival SS. Supplementation with aged garlic extract improves both NK and γδ-T cell function and reduces the severity of cold and flu symptoms: a randomized, double-blind, placebo-controlled nutrition intervention. Clin Nutr. 2012;31(3):337-44.

National Institute of Arthritis and Musculoskeletal and Skin Diseases. NIH osteoporosis and related bone diseases national resource center. *National Institute of Health*. http://www.niams.nih.gov/Health_Info/Bone/. Accessed January 3, 2014.

Ninan PT. The functional anatomy, neurochemistry, and pharmacology of anxiety. *J Clin Psychiatry*. 1999;60 Suppl 22:12-7.

Nishino H, Iwashima A, Itakura Y, Matsuura H, Fuwa T. Antitumor-promoting activity of garlic extracts. *Oncology*. 1989;46(4):277-80.

Nussey S, Whitehead SA. *Endocrinology: An Integrated Approach*. Oxford: BIOS;2001.

O'Keefe JH, Patil HR, Lavie CJ, Magalski A, Vogel RA, Mccullough PA. Potential adverse cardiovascular effects from excessive endurance exercise. *Mayo Clin Proc.* 2012;87(6):587-95.

Olpin M, Hesson M. *Stress Management for Life: A Research-Based Experiential Approach*. 3rd ed. Belmont, CA: Wadsworth, Cengage Learning;2013.

Paffenbarger RS, Hyde RT, Wing AL, Lee IM, Jung DL, Kampert JB. The association of changes in physical-activity level and other lifestyle characteristics with mortality among men. *N Engl J Med*. 1993;328(8):538-45.

Pappas S. No more FOFO: fear of missing out linked to dissatisfaction. *LiveScience*. http://www.livescience.com/31985-fear-missing-out-dissatisfaction.html. Accessed January 3, 2014.

Pelton R, LaValle JB, Hawkins EB. *Drug-Induced Nutrient Depletion Handbook*. 2nd ed. Hudson, OH: Lexi-Comp;2001.

Pfeiffer CC. *Mental and Elemental Nutrients*. New Canaan, CT: Keats Pub;1975.

Ploceniak C. [Bruxism and magnesium, my clinical experiences since 1980]. *Rev Stomatol Chir Maxillofac*. 1990;91 Suppl 1:127.

Punia S, Das M, Behari M, et al. Leads from xenobiotic metabolism genes for Parkinson's disease among north Indians. *Pharmacogenet Genomics*. 2011;21(12):790-7.

Quamme GA. Renal magnesium handling: new insights in understanding old problems. *Kidney Int*. 1997;52(5):1180-95.

Remer T, Manz F. Potential renal acid load of foods and its influence on urine pH. *J Am Diet Assoc*. 1995;95(7):791-7.

Ried K, Frank OR, Stocks NP. Aged garlic extract reduces blood pressure in hypertensives: a dose-response trial. *Eur J Clin Nutr*. 2013;67(1):64-70.

Rodger S. The 5 Pillars of Life: *Reclaiming Ownership of Your Mind, Body, and Future*. Ottawa, Canada: Core Systems Press;2005.

Rosanoff A, Seelig MS. Comparison of mechanism and functional effects of magnesium and statin pharmaceuticals. *J Am Coll Nutr*. 2004;23(5):501S-505S.

Rude RK, Singer FR, Gruber HE. Skeletal and hormonal effects of magnesium deficiency. *J Am Coll Nutr*. 2009;28(2):131-41.

Sartin JL, Kemppainen RJ, Coleman ES, Steele B, Williams JC. Cortisol inhibition of growth hormone-releasing hormone-stimulated growth hormone release from cultured sheep pituitary cells. *J Endocrinol*. 1994;141(3):517-25.

Sartori SB, Whittle N, Hetzenauer A, Singewald N. Magnesium deficiency induces anxiety and HPA axis dysregulation: modulation by therapeutic drug treatment. *Neuropharmacology*. 2012;62(1):304-12.

Sebastian A, Frassetto LA, Sellmeyer DE, Merriam RL, Morris RC. Estimation of the net acid load of the diet of ancestral preagricultural Homo sapiens and their hominid ancestors. *Am J Clin Nutr*. 2002;76(6):1308-16.

Serefko A, Szopa A, Wlaź P, et al. Magnesium in depression. *Pharmacol Rep*. 2013;65(3):547-54.

Song WJ, Chang YS. Magnesium sulfate for acute asthma in adults: a systematic literature review. *Asia Pac Allergy*. 2012;2(1):76-85.

Spasiov AA, Iezhitsa IN, Kharitonova MV, Kravchenko MS. [Pharmacological correction of pain sensitivity threshold in magnesium deficiency]. *Patol Fiziol Eksp Ter*. 2010;(1):6-10.

Steiner M, Li W. Aged garlic extract, a modulator of cardiovascular risk factors: a dose-finding study on the effects of AGE on platelet functions. *J Nutr*. 2001;131(3s):980S-4S.

Steventon GB, Heafield MT, Waring RH, Williams AC. Xenobiotic metabolism in Parkinson's disease. *Neurology.* 1989;39(7):883-7.

Steventon GB, Heafield MT, Sturman S, Waring RH, Williams AC. Xenobiotic metabolism in Alzheimer's disease. *Neurology.* 1990;40(7):1095-8.

Stewart PM, Toogood AA, Tomlinson JW. Growth hormone, insulin-like growth factor-I and the cortisol-cortisone shuttle. *Horm Res.* 2001;56 Suppl 1:1-6.

Stratakis CA. Cortisol and growth hormone: clinical implications of a complex, dynamic relationship. *Pediatr Endocrinol Rev.* 2006;3 Suppl 2:333-8.

Tanaka S, Haruma K, Kunihiro M, et al. Effects of aged garlic extract (AGE) on colorectal adenomas: a double-blinded study. *Hiroshima J Med Sci.* 2004;53(3-4):39-45.

Tang WH, Wang Z, Levison BS, et al. Intestinal microbial metabolism of phosphatidylcholine and cardiovascular risk. *N Engl J Med.* 2013;368(17):1575-84.

Time Inc. Your wireless life: results of Time's mobility poll. *Time.* http://content.time.com/time/interactive/0,31813,2122187,00.html. Accessed January 1, 2014.

Woodruff TJ, Zota AR, Schwartz JM. Environmental chemicals in pregnant women in the United States: NHANES 2003-2004. *Environ Health Perspect.* 2011;119(6):878-85.

Tudor-locke C, Bassett DR. How many steps/day are enough? Preliminary pedometer indices for public health. *Sports Med.* 2004;34(1):1-8.

Ushijima M, Sumioka I, Kakimoto M, et al. Effect of garlic and garlic preparations on physiological and psychological stress. *Phytother Res.* 1997;11(3):226–230.

Velichkovskiĭ BT. [Allergic diseases. Analysis of the causes of their increase]. *Vestn Akad Med Nauk SSSR.* 1991;(1):28-33.

Vrieze A, Holleman F, Zoetendal EG, De vos WM, Hoekstra JB, Nieuwdorp M. The environment within: how gut microbiota may influence metabolism and body composition. *Diabetologia.* 2010;53(4):606-13.

Werbach M, Moss J. *Textbook of Nutritional Medicine.* Tarzana, CA: Third Line Press;1999.

Wilson J. *Adrenal Fatigue: The 21st Century Stress Syndrome.* Petaluma, CA: Smart Publications;2001.

Wirth MM, Meier EA, Fredrickson BL, Schultheiss OC. Relationship between salivary cortisol and progesterone levels in humans. *Biol Psychol.* 2007;74(1):104-7.

Woodruff TJ, Zota AR, Schwartz JM. Environmental chemicals in pregnant women in the United States: NHANES 2003-2004. *Environ Health Perspect.* 2011;119(6):878-85.

World Health Organization, Food and Agriculture Organization of the United Nations. *Vitamin and Mineral Requirements in Human Nutrition.* 2nd ed. Geneva, Switzerland: World Health Organization;2005.

Zava DT, Blen M, Duwe G. Estrogenic activity of natural and synthetic estrogens in human breast cancer cells in culture. *Environ Health Perspect.* 1997;105 Suppl 3:637-45.

Zeb I, Ahmadi N, Nasir K, et al. Aged garlic extract and coenzyme Q10 have favorable effect on inflammatory markers and coronary atherosclerosis progression: a randomized clinical trial. *J Cardiovasc Dis Res.* 2012;3(3):185-90.

Index

About the Author

***

DANIEL CRISAFI, ND, PhD

BORN AND RAISED IN MONTRÉAL, Dr. Crisafi completed his postgraduate and graduate studies in the United States, and holds a doctorate in nutritional biochemistry, as well as a master herbalist degree.

Dr. Crisafi was a member of the advisory board of the Canadian Council of Continuing Education for Pharmacist's Power of Herbs course. He has also been part of the educational team of the Quebec endocrinologist's association. He is a former vice president and president of the board of directors of the École d'Enseignement Supérieur de Naturopathie du Québec and a former member of the advisory board of the Université Libre des Sciences de L'Homme de Paris. Dr. Crisafi has also served as vice chair on the Board of Directors for the Canadian Health Food Association (CHFA), which inducted him into its Hall of Fame in 2004.

Dr. Crisafi authored the first Canadian book on candidiasis (*Candida Albicans-EdiForma*) in 1987. He is also coauthor with Sam Graci of the book *Les Superaliments* (Chenelière McGraw-Hill). Dr. Crisafi contributed a chapter to Brad King and Michael A. Schmidt's book *Bio-Age: Ten Steps to a Younger You.*

Consultant for the health food and natural supplement industry for over 25 years, Dr. Crisafi is presently conducting postdoctoral research on the biochemical and physiological impact of stress. He has a private practice in Montreal, pH Santé Beauté.